M000073308

*[The Psalms] appear to me a mirror of the soul
of every one who sings them; they enable him to
perceive his own emotions, and to express them
in the words of the Psalms. . . . In its pages you
find portrayed man's whole life, the emotion of
his soul, and the frames of his mind.*

ATHANASIUS (C. 296-373)
BISHOP OF ALEXANDRIA

OTHER BOOKS BY JAMES W. SIRE

The Universe Next Door

Scripture Twisting

How to Read Slowly

The Discipleship of the Mind

Jesus the Reason

Chris Chrisman Goes to College

Why Should Anyone Believe Anything at All?

Habits of the Mind

Václav Havel

Naming the Elephant: Worldview as a Concept

Learning to Pray Through the Psalms

Why Good Arguments Often Fail

A Little Primer on Humble Apologetics

Praying the
Psalms of Jesus

JAMES W. SIRE

IVP Books

An imprint of InterVarsity Press
Downers Grove, Illinois

InterVarsity Press
P.O. Box 1400, Downers Grove, IL 60515-1426
World Wide Web: www.ivpress.com
E-mail: email@ivpress.com

©2007 by James W. Sire

All rights reserved. No part of this book may be reproduced in any form without written permission from InterVarsity
Press.

InterVarsity Press® is the book-publishing division of InterVarsity Christian Fellowship/USA®, a student movement
active on campus at hundreds of universities, colleges and schools of nursing in the United States of America,
and a member movement of the International Fellowship of Evangelical Students. For information about local and
regional activities, write Public Relations Dept., InterVarsity Christian Fellowship/USA, 6400 Schroeder Rd.,
P.O. Box 7895, Madison, WI 53707-7895, or visit the IVCF website at <www.intervarsity.org>.

Scripture quotations, unless otherwise noted, are from the New Revised Standard Version of the Bible, copyright
1989 by the Division of Christian Education of the National Council of the Churches of Christ in the USA. Used by
permission. All rights reserved.

Design: Cindy Kiple
Images: Denis Waugh/Getty Images

ISBN 978-0-8308-3508-9

Printed in the United States of America ∞

Library of Congress Cataloging-in-Publication Data

Sire, James W.
  Praying the Psalms of Jesus / James W. Sire.
      p. cm.
  Includes bibliographical references and index.
  ISBN 978-0-8308-3508-9 (pbk.: alk. paper)
  1. Bible. O.T. Psalms—Criticism, interpretation, etc. 2. Jesus
Christ. I. Title.
  BS1430.52.S57 2007
  223'.206—dc22

                                                                                      2007021559

| P | 19 | 18 | 17 | 16 | 15 | 14 | 13 | 12 | 11 | 10 | 9 | 8 | 7 | 6 | 5 | 4 | 3 | 2 | 1 |
| Y | 23 | 22 | 21 | 20 | 19 | 18 | 17 | 16 | 15 | 14 | 13 | 12 | 11 | 10 | 09 | 08 | 07 |

To Marj

Contents

Acknowledgments

The origin of this book is, of course, the Old Testament psalms themselves. Their impact on my life has been immeasurable. I have come to think in their phrases, meditate on their images and see life itself in terms of their concepts. So I thank the Lord who inspired his poets, liturgists and prophets to conceive and compose the great and wonderful Psalter.

A second rank of thanks goes to the many scholars, teachers and translators who have made the psalms accessible for prayer and meditation. Among them I want to single out scholars Derek Kidner, Peter Craggie and Pius Drijvers whose commentaries have been especially helpful to me. Eugene Peterson should be mentioned for his concept of *answering speech,* Michael Wilcock for his clear exposition and Charles Spurgeon for his eloquent reflections.

But whom should I thank for the specific stimulus for this book? I think it must be the psalmist David himself (or whoever composed Psalm 22), for it is this psalm that lies at the heart of my understanding of the psalms of the ancients and the psalms of Jesus. Some twenty years ago I preached my first psalm-inspired sermon with Psalm 22 as the text, and I have preached it many times since. It was, however, Dietrich Bonhoeffer and Thomas Merton who convinced me that every psalm is a psalm of Jesus. This knowledge has transformed the way I now read and meditate on every psalm. I am pleased to acknowledge as well two scholar-readers of the manuscript. I am not supposed to know who they are, so I will not name them, but, dear scholars, I do know who you are and I thank you!

I'd love also to thank those who helped me move this book from notes to manuscript and from manuscript to book. First among them is my wife, Marjorie, who has corrected so many typos, outright spelling errors and grammatical goofs that I am embarrassed to count them. She is my first line of defense against myself. Second are my editor, Cindy Bunch, as well as my longtime theological and biblical scholar-friend Jim Hoover at InterVarsity Press. Finally, Ruth Goring as copyeditor identifies my stylistic peccadillos and generously puts up with them or amends and polishes them.

With these acknowledgments I think I have successfully avoided taking any blame for any erors remaining. Oops!

James W. Sire
March 2007

INTRODUCTION

Knowing Jesus by Praying the Psalms

"My God, my God, why have you forsaken me?"

Hᴏw deeply into the mind and heart of another can one penetrate? How much can we know about anyone other than ourselves? Can we even know ourselves?

We are blessed with consciousness. "We think, therefore we are," we may say with Descartes. But our own thoughts remain ours. Who we think we are is utterly private. We cannot let people into our mind even when we want to. The essence of who we are lies too deep for words.

Better, we must admit, too deep for words lies each self even to itself. Who can say they know who they are? Too deep and too mysterious, too distant and too foggy, too encrusted by false consciousness, too darkened by sin, we hide from and are hidden from clear self-knowledge.

What we need is a view from the outside by the only One who knows who we are. We need a voice *sub species eternitatus,* a voice from eternity. This is precisely what we get from Scripture. God talks to us through the voices of his prophets, through the witness of the Holy Spirit through Scripture, through the words of Jesus, his disciples and those who have told his story through the Gospels. For all this we are amazed, we thank God, and we steep ourselves in his Word.

What may be more amazing is that God speaks to us through the voices of the psalmists—those ancient men of yore who, having heard the Word of the Lord in the seething caldron of their own life and times, answered back. Their answering speech becomes for us a primary clue to who we are. It pulls the mask from our ego, lays bare our soul and shows us the glory and wretchedness of our own existence. As John Calvin says, the psalms are a mirror of the soul,

> for there is not an emotion of which one may become conscious that is not represented as in a mirror. Or rather, the Holy Spirit has here drawn to the life all the griefs, sorrows, fears, doubts, hopes, cares, perplexities, in short, all the distracting emotions with which the minds of men are wont to be agitated. . . . It is by perusing those inspired compositions, that men will be most effectually awakened to a sense of their maladies, and, at the same time, instructed in seeking remedies for their cure. In a word, whatever may serve to encourage us when we are about to pray to God is taught us in this book.

More amazing yet—and this will be a central thesis of this book—the psalms give us an insight into God himself, especially as manifested in our Lord Jesus Christ, the incarnate Son of God. When we absorb the psalms, when they become our own answering speech, we participate in the mind of Christ, not because we have ourselves risen to the level of the Godhead but because Jesus himself prayed the psalms.

Through the psalms, then, we come to know both who God is and who we are. A deep journey through the psalms is daunting. When we see who we are, it may shake us to our roots. When we see who God is, it may send us spinning through the cosmos to the foothills of heaven itself, where, like Isaiah, we may see God "sitting on the throne, high and lifted up," or, like the apostle John, see "one like the Son of Man" with eyes "like a flame of fire" and a voice "like the sound of many waters" (Isaiah 6:1; Revelation 1:13-15).

THE MIND AND HEART OF JESUS

At key moments in his life on earth Jesus Christ, the very Son of God, turned to the psalms for words to express his deepest thoughts and emotions. The most noted and well-known of these is, of course, Jesus' cry of dereliction on the cross: "My God, my God, why have you forsaken me?" (Matthew 27:46). But also in the Garden of Gethsemane, Jesus echoed the refrain of Psalm 42, as he said to his three closest disciples, "I am deeply grieved, even unto death" (Psalm 42:5, 7, 11; 43:5; Mark 14:34). Likewise during the Last Supper, Jesus announced to his disciples that "to fulfill the scripture, 'The one who ate my bread has lifted his heel against me'" (Psalm 41:9; John 13:18).

It is not hard to imagine Jesus, his mind and heart saturated with the words and thoughts of the psalms, going off alone early in the morning to pray. How often must he have mouthed the words of the psalms and given them a fulfillment that none had ever given them before or ever would again? They became his answering speech to his heavenly Father.

This is what I desire for this set of studies in the Psalms. I want the psalms that relate closely to the mission and mind of Jesus to become our answering speech. And I want us to realize that in a very important sense every psalm is a psalm of Jesus and a psalm for us as well.

These studies continue the approach of *Learning to Pray Through the Psalms,* though it is not necessary to have used that book to use this one. The goal of the first book was (1) to learn what the psalms say about and do with prayer, (2) to learn to pray by means of the psalmist's words and (3) to develop a way of praying psalms together with others. The goal of this book is similar, with two important further goals: (4) to explicitly focus on the heart and mind of Jesus as he prayed the psalms and (5) to suggest how by praying the psalms of Jesus we can gain insight into the human life of our Lord and Savior.

EVERY PSALM A PSALM OF JESUS

A bit of my own engagement in the psalms may help explain why I find the psalms so rich. I have been reading, living with and in some sense praying the psalms for over fifty years. *Learning to Pray Through the Psalms* was one result. Moreover, I have long known that some of them were quoted by Jesus. So I thought that I would try to understand both Jesus and the psalms better by focusing on those he referred to or were associated with him by various writers of the New Testament.

As I pondered the psalms and read scholars, however, I came recently to the conclusion that all the psalms were Jesus' own. All of them—the beautiful and the ugly, the glorious and the grim, the plain and the elaborate, the blessings and the curses: every single one of them has been filtered through his heart and mind. Indeed, *every psalm is a psalm of Jesus.* While Jesus did not put it quite this way, did he not say this to his disciples just before his ascension? "These are the words that I spoke to you while I was still with you—that everything written about me in the law of Moses, the prophets, and the psalms must be fulfilled" (Luke 24:44; see also v. 27).

How can this be? C. S. Lewis, the twentieth century's most honored Christian scholar, once wrote, "In some of the Psalms the spirit of hatred which strikes us in the face is like the heat from a furnace mouth. In others the same spirit ceases to be frightful only by becoming (to a modern mind) almost comic in its naivety."

Hatred, naiveté—surely our Lord and Savior did not harbor such rancor, such detachment from reality! No, but he knew what people are like. As the incarnate Son of God, Jesus knew the depths of people's sinfulness in at least two ways: first by his life with them, then by the rich lode of human nature revealed in the psalms and other Scriptures. As a young boy, "Jesus increased in wisdom and in years, and in divine and human favor" (Luke 2:52). As theologian Thomas C. Oden says, "He was willing to undergo gradual human development so that he could share fully in all the ordinary stages of human growth (Luke 2:40, cf. 1 Sam 2:26). . . . Thus the eternal Son, in humbling himself to share in the human condition, went through an education; he studied, listened attentively, learned obedience (Heb 5:8), and was taught by degrees to pray, to read, to meditate on Holy Writ, serving a real apprenticeship as a carpenter." Through active participation in the rites of Israel, Jesus would have become intimately familiar with the Psalms. For at the time of Christ, "the Psalter took its final form as the hymn book . . . as an integral part of the worship of the postexilic community."

The Psalms and, in general, the liturgy of the Hebrews display the full range of human emotions, human dreams, human love and hatred. Jesus knew the psalms. As biblical scholar Graeme Goldsworthy says, "Jesus used the Psalms in prayer, and as a source of authoritative teaching." More important, "he saw himself as fulfilling certain aspects of the Psalms, especially in his passion," as we will see in the opening chapter of this book. In fact, "he is recorded as using the Psalms more than any other Old Testament book."

What, then, is the relationship between Jesus and the Psalms? Did Jesus get his idea of who he was from them, or did he know intuitively who he was and then reveal to his disciples what the ultimate meaning of these psalms is? New Testament scholar Ben Witherington III is not sure: "It is hard to say whether Jesus' self-understanding affected more the way he looked at these texts, or the texts themselves affected more how Jesus viewed himself and his mission." If we take seriously the humanity of Jesus and his participation in the way human beings learn, I am inclined to think that he came to understand himself at least partly through the ability of his own Holy-Spirit-inspired, sin-free mind to read the Scriptures and to understand them like no one before him.

All of this, of course, does not explain how the awe-filled but awful passages in the Psalms could reflect the mind and heart of the very Son of God. Psalm 22, however, provides, so it seems to me, more than a clue. If Jesus could absorb and declare to his Father, "I am a worm" (v. 6), if the incarnate Son of God could feel utterly abandoned by God the Father, then the worst of human thoughts and emotions could well become his own. Perhaps they must become his own, else he cannot bear their burden and take their consequences. Goldsworthy agrees: "All Old Testament texts point to Christ. Those that deal with human sin testify to the sinful nature that was imputed to Jesus in his death on the cross."

Until we deal with the imprecation, the cursing, in specific psalms, let us let Dietrich Bonhoeffer have the last word on this topic:

It is the incarnate Son of God, who has borne every human
weakness in his own flesh, who here pours out the heart of all
humanity before God and who stands in our place and prays
for us. He has known torment and pain, guilt and death more
deeply than we. Therefore it is the prayer of the human nature
assumed by him which comes before God. It is really our
prayer, but since he knows us better than we know ourselves
and since he himself was true man for our sakes, it is also really
his prayer, and it can become our prayer only because it was
his prayer.

When we pray the psalms of Jesus, the wisdom of Bonhoeffer becomes obvious.

FOUR LAST WORDS OF JESUS

How deeply did the psalms enter into Jesus' mind and heart? The answer is striking. So deeply had he pondered the psalms that four of
the traditional "seven last words" (seven last sentences) of Jesus on the
cross were quotations from or allusions to the Psalms. Each of the
seven words reflects the poignancy of the moment within the compass
of time and eternity. The first three concern the people immediately
around him. They display Jesus' compassion not only for his mother
and the disciples but also—and first—for the very people who were
responsible for his death or who were worthy of death themselves.

1. "Father, forgive them; for they do not know what they are doing"
   (to the people who were mocking and crucifying him; Luke
   23:34).

2. "Truly I tell you, today you will be with me in Paradise" (to the
   thief who confessed his faults and asked for Jesus' mercy; Luke
   23:43).

3. "Woman, here is your son" (to his mother Mary). "Here is your mother" (to "the disciple whom he loved," probably John; John 19:26-27).

The final four concern Jesus himself and his relation to God the Father. It is striking that when Jesus turned from those around him and to his Father God, he chose psalms as his voice.

4. "Eloi, Eloi, lema sabachthani," that is, "My God, my God, why have you forsaken me?" (Mark 15:34 and Matthew 27:46, quoting Psalm 22:1).

5. "I am thirsty" (John 19:28, quoting Psalm 69:21; cf. 22:15).

6. "It is finished" (John 19:30, quoting Psalm 22:31).

7. "Father, into your hands I commend my spirit" (Luke 23:46, alluding to Psalm 31:5).

Indeed, all the psalms are psalms of Jesus, but some of them penetrated and informed his consciousness more than others. This book examines and prays all of the more important of these. But there are many other psalms that deserve to be examined in the light of Jesus' life and ministry. It is my hope that with the encouragement of this book, you and other readers will begin to take advantage of the great lode of wisdom, psychological realism and spiritual insight afforded by the Psalter.

STRUCTURE OF THE BOOK

It may help to understand the structure of this book. In part one, "Jesus in the Psalms," we begin our journey into the mind of Christ by immersing ourselves in several psalms that Jesus himself refers to and fulfills (Psalm 22; 110; 118; 2 and 69). Then, since in the final analysis every psalm in the Psalter is a psalm of Jesus, in part two, "The Psalms in Jesus," we will immerse ourselves in psalms that are usually not considered directly messianic (Psalm 29; 23; 45 and 80).

For private reading and praying: Most of this book concentrates on private reading and praying. Following the explanation of each psalm, therefore, is a private liturgy—one way of making each psalm your own answering speech to God.

For corporate prayer: But the psalms can and should also be prayed in community. In Israel many of the psalms were used in community worship. Today they are still used in the liturgies and prayer books of many denominations. That's why each chapter includes a guide for group study and a liturgy, a "directed prayer," to focus the thoughts and yearnings of a group for a closer fellowship with each other and with God. If the specific words of the directed prayer do not fit your group, don't hesitate to adjust them. There are many ways to pray the psalms in community. This is just one of them.

We begin with the most poignant and powerful of the psalms of Jesus—Psalm 22.

PART ONE

Jesus in the Psalms

JESUS, ABANDONED AND EXALTED

Psalm 22

There is an infinite abyss in the human heart that can only be filled by God himself." So wrote Blaise Pascal. Augustine had said the same thing centuries before: "Our heart is restless until it rests in you."

The truth of these words is written on our soul, whether we know it or not. Those who have met God understand these words even before they hear them. What happens, then, when suddenly we feel that God has left us? How do we respond? We can know right now, before we even read Psalm 22, that we are not alone in feeling alone.

"My God, my God, why have you forsaken me?" These words uttered by Jesus as he hung on the cross must be the most agonized cry ever to be uttered by a man—a man whom we understand was and still is the Son of God. The Son of God abandoned by God the Father: is this what these words mean?

Or do we see these words as only the cry of the human Jesus, a person solely like us, who seems to lose his intimate contact with God? Are they the only thing the agonized man could at that time remember from his understanding of Scripture? Could they ever be uttered by

us? Should they ever be uttered by us? These are the poignant puzzles
we encounter as we try to understand and to pray Psalm 22.

The psalms of Jesus—those he took into himself and declared his
own—give us a keen insight into Jesus' mind and heart. They also
serve as mirrors of our own soul. That is nowhere more clear than in
Psalm 22. So we will begin with this psalm.

In one sense we begin at the end, for this is one of the psalms that
Jesus quoted near the end of his life. In another sense, we begin at
the beginning because understanding this psalm and the part it
played in Jesus' life, death and resurrection becomes a key to understanding all the psalms from Jesus' point of view.

INITIAL READING OF PSALM 22

The first requisite for understanding a psalm—or any other literary
text—is to read it carefully. That means to read it over and over, to
read it till its words and music, its images and themes, its emotions
and notions sink deeply into both your conscious and your subconscious self. So each chapter begins with a psalm and an invitation to
read it with such care before proceeding with the remainder of the
chapter. My intent is not so much to convince you that my particular
reading is correct as for you to look for yourself and to come along
with me as I try to open up the psalm—to clarify its multiple meanings and to help it become your own answering speech to God.

PSALM 22

Plea for Deliverance from Suffering and Hostility

To the leader: according to The Deer of the Dawn. A Psalm of David.

^{1}My God, my God, why have you forsaken me?
  Why are you so far from helping me, from the words of my
    groaning?

²O my God, I cry by day, but you do not answer;
　　and by night, but find no rest.
³Yet you are holy,
　　enthroned on the praises of Israel.
⁴In you our ancestors trusted;
　　they trusted, and you delivered them.
⁵To you they cried, and were saved;
　　in you they trusted, and were not put to shame.

⁶But I am a worm, and not human;
　　scorned by others, and despised by the people.
⁷All who see me mock at me;
　　they make mouths at me, they shake their heads;
⁸"Commit your cause to the LORD; let him deliver—
　　let him rescue the one in whom he delights!"

⁹Yet it was you who took me from the womb;
　　you kept me safe on my mother's breast.
¹⁰On you I was cast from my birth,
　　and since my mother bore me you have been my God.
¹¹Do not be far from me,
　　for trouble is near
　　and there is no one to help.

¹²Many bulls encircle me,
　　strong bulls of Bashan surround me;
¹³they open wide their mouths at me,
　　like a ravening and roaring lion.

¹⁴I am poured out like water,
　　and all my bones are out of joint;
　my heart is like wax;

it is melted within my breast;
¹⁵my mouth is dried up like a potsherd,
   and my tongue sticks to my jaws;
   you lay me in the dust of death.

¹⁶For dogs are all around me;
   a company of evildoers encircles me.
 My hands and feet have shriveled;
¹⁷I can count all my bones.
 They stare and gloat over me;
¹⁸they divide my clothes among themselves,
   and for my clothing they cast lots.

¹⁹But you, O LORD, do not be far away!
   O my help, come quickly to my aid!
²⁰Deliver my soul from the sword,
   my life from the power of the dog!
²¹   Save me from the mouth of the lion!

 From the horns of the wild oxen you have rescued me.
²²I will tell of your name to my brothers and sisters;
   in the midst of the congregation I will praise you:
²³You who fear the LORD, praise him!
   All you offspring of Jacob, glorify him;
   stand in awe of him, all you offspring of Israel!
²⁴For he did not despise or abhor
   the affliction of the afflicted;
 he did not hide his face from me,
   but heard when I cried to him.

²⁵From you comes my praise in the great congregation;
   my vows I will pay before those who fear him.

[26]The poor shall eat and be satisfied;
>   those who seek him shall praise the LORD.
>   May your hearts live forever!

[27]All the ends of the earth shall remember
>   and turn to the LORD;
>   and all the families of the nations
>   shall worship before him.
[28]For dominion belongs to the LORD,
>   and he rules over the nations.

[29]To him, indeed, shall all who sleep in the earth bow down;
>   before him shall bow all who go down to the dust,
>   and I shall live for him.
[30]Posterity will serve him;
>   future generations will be told about the LORD,
[31]and proclaim his deliverance to a people yet unborn,
>   saying that he has done it.

FARTHER OUT AND FURTHER IN

If we have read Psalm 22 with the care it deserves, we are sure to
come away with a profound sense of both the agony and the ecstasy
of the psalmist, for Psalm 22 begins in the most awesome cry of dereliction in all of literature and it ends in one of its most ecstatic ex-
postulations. We should come away from such reading struck with
awe, for we have just been treading on holy ground. If we have not
yet sensed this, we should read and reread it until we do. Still we
have only just begun.

Grasping Psalm 22 begins with careful reading, but it does not
end there. To enter the psalm, we need to go both farther out and
further in. In going out we must see the psalm in its multiple con-

texts—its relation to its author, then to his community, then to its
place in the life of Jesus and finally its significance to us. In going
in, we must analyze both its overall rational structure (how it moves
in idea from beginning to end) and its emotional structure (how
and why the emotions displayed change—if they do—from beginning to end). We must understand any obscure references to people, places and events, and reflect on the images or metaphors that
take us deeper into the psalmist's mind or vision of reality. Finally,
in an act of comprehensive imagination, we must try to see the
psalm as a single whole, enfolding it into our mind and heart. We
are not looking for the sum of its parts but the essence of its whole-
ness. Let us begin.

THE FOUR CONTEXTS OF PSALM 22

Context 1: Psalm 22 is titled "A Psalm of David." Scholars generally
believe that the psalms that bear this designation could well have
been written by him; if not, they were written under his influence or
in his court, so to speak. Though this psalm may have stemmed from
a particular incident in David's life, it gives away no details. It does,
however, provide an insight into David's experience and his sense of
being abandoned by God.

Context 2: David's psalms became an important part of the liturgy
of the Hebrews, and thus David the psalmist became the voice of Israel. This means that the lament of the opening verses is just as much
a lament of Israel as of David.

Context 3: The opening line of Psalm 22 became one of the "seven
last words of Christ" as he hung on the cross on Golgotha. This fact,
plus multiple references to events that transpired while Jesus was being crucified, lifts the whole psalm to a new, prophetic level. Verse 1
cries out for special attention, as Jesus took it for his own. It is the

very voice of Jesus. In fact, the whole psalm, even the final phrase of verse 31, is his voice.

Context 4: After the death and resurrection of Jesus, all the psalms became a part of the liturgy of the early church and have remained to this day part the worship experience of both the liturgical and the nonliturgical churches. They remain the answering speech of individual worshipers and their communities. If we appropriate it, therefore, Psalm 22 will be our answering speech as well.

RATIONAL AND EMOTIONAL STRUCTURES

The flow of ideas and emotions in Psalm 22 is complex and, in some ways, a puzzle. The lament itself comes in three phases, each of which includes a countercharge. A prayer follows both the second and the third phases. The first phase is the most emotionally intense. The psalmist cries out that God has utterly abandoned him. Still with increasingly distressing images, each succeeding phase fleshes out the agony. Then suddenly, not only is there no more lament but the psalmist declares the problem solved and praises God, finally blurting out, "It's all over. God has done it!"

The following outline makes this structure obvious.

Lament 1: You, God, have abandoned me, verses 1-2
Countercharge: But you weren't like this in the past, verses 3-5

Lament 2: I am subhuman, to others an object of disgust, verses 6-8
Countercharge 2: You used to care for me, verses 9-10
Prayer 1: Come to me, verse 11

Lament 3: I am besieged by enemies and utterly desolate, verses 12-18
Prayer 2: Come and save me, verses 19-21a
[Radical break. Events happen offstage.]

Ecstatic praise: You have saved me. I praise you and call others to do so too, verses 21b-24

Prophecy in hope: You have solved all humankind's problems. Everyone will praise you, verses 25-31

I know of few psalms—or for that matter few poems of any kind—in which the radical reversal in emotions is so sudden, so dramatic, so unexpected, so unprepared for by what has preceded it. If it were not for their fulfillment in Jesus on the cross, verses 21b-31 would be utterly unreasonable. Look at the psalm from the standpoint of the four voices, that is, the four contexts.

First, if the psalm is read as a lament of King David (or any individual ancient psalmist), the ecstasy is unmerited, the praise is far out of proportion. David has a problem. He feels that he has been abandoned. Fair enough—easy enough to understand. So he makes his lament, in essence calling out three times, "How long, O Lord, are you going to keep me feeling this way?" Then, between verse 21a and 21b (offstage, so to speak), God comes to David. He is no longer utterly alone. Now he calls first on all of Israel, the great congregation, to rejoice. Then, because God has delivered him, he sees that all the nations will rejoice, all the living and all the dead; in other words, everyone everywhere for all of time. All this just because God brought David out of his despair!

Aren't we entitled to say, "Good grief, David, get a grip! You're not that big a deal!"

Okay, so David is not the only voice. There is also the voice of Israel: an entire nation of people has been delivered. Still, this is not enough to elicit such extensive praise. From any point of view, Israel has always been only one tiny nation, one tiny people, among a host of nations and peoples. The ecstasy is still too great, over the top.

Of course, there is your voice and my voice. This psalm can be our answering speech too. Isn't that enough? Hardly. Okay. Then combine it with the voices of succeeding Hebrew generations and the voices of the churches throughout the ages. Is this enough? It's getting closer. But I think not.

Finally, there is the voice of Jesus. Only his voice justifies both the rational and the emotional structure of the psalm. Think of this psalm as what T. S. Eliot called an *objective correlative,* in this case an objective correlative of the mind and heart of Jesus—a way of verbalizing in fully human language a divine revelation of what could not be directly stated. Or put it this way: Jesus fulfilled the pattern of thought and emotion that David captured in his own overstated way in Psalm 22, and made his statement truer than David ever could have imagined. Psalm 22:1-21a reveals the mind and heart of Jesus as he took on himself the sins that separated him from the Father. Verses 21b-31 call for the praise due to God the Father who did not allow his holy one to "see the Pit" (Psalm 16:10). Psalm 22, then, encompasses three key elements of the gospel—the atonement, the resurrection and the ascension—and sets them in the realistic context of human desperation.

The final phrase of the final verse ("he has done it") is the clincher. On the cross, Jesus reflects on this verse as he receives the sour wine, and he says, "It is finished" (John 19:30). No wonder Psalm 22 ends in ecstasy!

PROPHETIC DETAIL

Is Psalm 22 a prophecy? Did David believe that he was forecasting the crucifixion of the Son of God? Of course, we will never know the answer, at least to the second question. But I doubt it. Rather, I think David was reflecting on his own experience and by extension perhaps the experience of Israel. It is just that this experience is itself paradigmatic of the experience of all people everywhere when they recognize the truth of the human situation. If we could see ourselves as God sees us, we would realize that apart from the grace of God, we are not only separated from God at the moment but have no hope of ever being able to stand in his presence. It is indeed better that God has left us, for if he were here in his fullness and we were still in our sins, we would be eternally crushed by the weight of his glory.

David knew that. Yet David was also a man after God's own heart (Acts 13:22). While he might with the apostle Paul say that he was the chief of sinners (a murderer, an adulterer, a thief), he also trusted God for forgiveness (Psalm 51).

The opening line of Psalm 22 is David's voice. Inspired by the Holy Spirit, it is also the voice of Israel, all nations and all humanity. And as the Son of God became incarnate and took on our sins, he became the voice not just of verse 1 but of the whole psalm.

So too with the details that have so fascinated Christian readers of the Gospels. They are the metaphoric and, some of them, even the literal details of the crucifixion. Here are the literal in chart form:

Verse 1	Mark 15:34	the cry of dereliction
	Matthew 27:46	
Verses 7-8	Mark 15:16-20	mocking soldiers
	Matthew 27:31, 38-44	
	Luke 23:36	
	Mark 15:29-32	mocking people, priests
	Luke 23:35	
	Luke 23:39	mocking criminal
Verses 14	John 19:28	thirst
Verse 18	Mark 15:24	dividing the garments and casting
	Luke 23:34	lots
	John 19:23-25	
Verse 31	John 19:30	he has done it / it is finished

In addition to these literal embodiments of David's vision, the graphic details of verses 14-15 seem like a photograph of Jesus hanging on the cross.

> ¹⁴I am poured out like water,
>> and all my bones are out of joint;
> my heart is like wax;
>> it is melted within my breast;
> ¹⁵my mouth is dried up like a potsherd,
>> and my tongue sticks to my jaws;
>> you lay me in the dust of death.

The details fit hand in glove with what Jesus must have been experiencing. Likewise David's metaphors for his taunters—bulls of Bashan, dog, lion and wild oxen—are universal, as relevant for Jesus and us as they were for David.

MAKING THE PSALM OUR OWN

How, then, can we truly make Psalm 22 our own? I believe that we can do this in two stages.

First, as much as we can, we should see the psalm through the mind and heart of the ancient psalmist and the community of Israel. There is little in the psalm with which we cannot empathize, for we too sometimes sense the absence of God, the God in whom we used to find comfort and whose presence we sensed in our ordinary life as well as our worship. Each of us as individuals and our community as well have experienced the presence of God. But there are times when he seems so far away, and we don't understand why. At times we too are beset by "strong bulls of Bashan" who ridicule us because we believe that God could really have some relevance to how we all got here. We read that well-known scientists like Richard Dawkins say such things as "It is absolutely safe to say that if you meet somebody who claims not to believe in evolution, that person is ignorant, stupid, or insane (or wicked, but I'd rather not consider that)." Our whole culture has become a battlefield of ideas, and we often seem to be on the losing side. Where is God in all of this? We, David and ancient Israel inhabit essentially the same world.

There is, however, one major difference. We know that on the cross Jesus quoted the opening line of the psalm and made it his own. This forever lifts the psalm out of ancient Israel and places it in the center of history, the point at which God in Christ is reconciling the world to himself. To make this psalm our own, we need to see it as Christ saw it. And he saw it as the *objective correlative* of his atoning sacrifice. He was bearing the burden of our sins. He was dying—being separated from God the Father—in our place. He was "made . . . to be sin who knew no sin, so that in him we might become the righteousness of God" (2 Corinthians 5:21). So as we read and pray this psalm, we should consciously see Christ on the cross, bearing our sin. Then, as the psalm turns to ecstatic praise, we rejoice with the risen Christ and see ourselves as part of the gigantic Christian community now praising God as a further fulfillment of the prophetic character of verses 27-31. With an inner shout—if not an outer expostulation—we finally declare, "Christ has done it! It is finished!" The agony of the opening line and the immersion in the troubling images and frustrated reflection ceases. And our heart turns to pure joy!

PRAYING PSALM 22

When we have made the psalm our own, we are ready to turn to prayer. So read through the entire psalm again. Then with eyes open read and pray section by section.

¹My God, my God, why have you forsaken me?
　　Why are you so far from helping me, from the words of my
　　　　groaning?
²O my God, I cry by day, but you do not answer;
　　and by night, but find no rest.

Respond: Lord, I come to you now. The words of David and Jesus, the ancient Hebrews and the church down through the ages are on my lips. At this point in my life I do not sense your absence, but I do begin to understand why David might have done so. For there are times when I too have been discouraged, times when I was so depressed that I could not even mouth these lines. *If you are now in such a state, simply let these first two verses be your own desperate prayer.*

But in my prayer now, let me join David in crying out to you for all those who are in despair. For those who are your children, you are not just any God, not just the transcendent God beyond the sky, the very God of very God; to them and to me, you are "my God, my God." They cry out to you. You do not seem to answer. By day they walk in a world that seems empty of love and care. By night they toss and turn and find no rest.

Father, what was it like for your only begotten Son? So much more agony must have been his. He bore my sin and suffered your absence. He died. He died for the sins of the world. He died for me. *Pause in silence for a few minutes as you meditate on what Jesus did for all his children.*

Lord Jesus, thank you! You did for me what I and no one else could do. Your grace is sufficient for me. Thank you, Jesus! *Pause in silence.*

Holy Spirit, bore into me the greatness of the gift of salvation that cost the holy Trinity so much.

³Yet you are holy,
    enthroned on the praises of Israel.
⁴In you our ancestors trusted;
    they trusted, and you delivered them.
⁵To you they cried, and were saved;
    in you they trusted, and were not put to shame.

Respond: David knew the stories of the Torah. He knew about the patriarchs and Moses, the Egyptian captivity and the exodus, the already long history of his people. You were worthy of David's trust, yet he felt you had abandoned him. And Jesus, whose sweet communion with you characterized his whole life, he who said to those who thought him mad, "I and the Father are one"—he now senses your absence. How deeply? *Pause in silence.*

⁶But I am a worm, and not human;
    scorned by others, and despised by the people.
⁷All who see me mock at me;
    they make mouths at me, they shake their heads;
⁸"Commit your cause to the LORD; let him deliver—
    let him rescue the one in whom he delights!"

Respond: Lord, that David could call himself a worm I can understand. I have almost thought that about myself. *Think of the times when you have been depressed, and lay them before the Lord now. Then think of Jesus.* But Jesus? Could the Son of God, very God of very God, feel this way? Could it be that this feeling was a part of his bearing our sin? Could this sense of worthlessness be the sin itself— our sin—as it came pressing down on the eternally God-conscious Son of God, who had now become sin for us? The mystery of the atonement is too much for me to unravel. But could this be a glimpse behind the veil that separates us from the Godhead? *Pause in silence.*

[9]Yet it was you who took me from the womb;
    you kept me safe on my mother's breast.
[10]On you I was cast from my birth,
    and since my mother bore me you have been my God.

Respond: Thank you, Lord, my protector from the beginning! Thank you, too, for David's knowing this truth and remembering it under duress. Even if it heightened his distress, it was a truth that fit. And Jesus, whose birth we celebrate each year: Father God, he too knew of the love of Mary and your love as he grew into manhood.

[11]Do not be far from me,
        for trouble is near
        and there is no one to help.

Respond: Lord, in our sense of distance from you, there is nothing else to do but ask you to show yourself. We need you. You are our only hope. But you are so far away. Look, Lord:

[12]Many bulls encircle me,
        strong bulls of Bashan surround me;
[13]they open wide their mouths at me,
        like a ravening and roaring lion.

[14]I am poured out like water,
        and all my bones are out of joint;
    my heart is like wax;
        it is melted within my breast;
[15]my mouth is dried up like a potsherd,
        and my tongue sticks to my jaws;
        you lay me in the dust of death.

¹⁶For dogs are all around me;

>   a company of evildoers encircles me.

>   My hands and feet have shriveled;

¹⁷I can count all my bones.

>   They stare and gloat over me;

¹⁸they divide my clothes among themselves,

>   and for my clothing they cast lots.

Respond: Lord, in this longest lament of David's and Jesus' prayer, you still have not come. Where are you? What are you doing? I see David attacked by his enemies, the enemies of ancient Israel. Where are you? I see him languishing not just in mind but in body too. And Jesus, flogged and bleeding, with soldiers casting lots for his clothes, yet still forgiving his tormentors, comforting his mother, giving assurance to a thief who hangs by his side, and then saying, "I thirst." By his mercy and grace, it is I who hang there, or rather, it is Jesus *as me* who hangs there. In my mind I cry with David and Jesus:

¹⁹But you, O LORD, do not be far away!

>   O my help, come quickly to my aid!

²⁰Deliver my soul from the sword,

>   my life from the power of the dog!

²¹ Save me from the mouth of the lion!

Respond: Lord, the intensity of David's and Jesus' lament is here matched by the intensity of their prayer. It is their final plea, and we know it will be answered. David too knows it by faith, and Jesus must have known it more directly. But in the brutal crisis of body and mind, they live in desperate hope, projecting the certainty of their faith by the urgency of their request. Thanks be to you! You came. And they and all of us have rejoiced and will rejoice.

From the horns of the wild oxen you have rescued me.
²²I will tell of your name to my brothers and sisters;
    in the midst of the congregation I will praise you:
²³You who fear the LORD, praise him!
    All you offspring of Jacob, glorify him;
    stand in awe of him, all you offspring of Israel!
²⁴For he did not despise or abhor
    the affliction of the afflicted;
  he did not hide his face from me,
    but heard when I cried to him.

Respond: Let the ecstasy begin! I can do no better than repeat these verses. *Repeat verses 21b-24 several times.* May I do as David: tell of the goodness of your presence, the blessing of your deliverance. He did so in the words of this psalm, and millions have been blessed. May I continue in his tradition. The Son of God came and made you known, Father, in ways David could not imagine. May I follow them in declaring your glory to my friends and anyone who will listen!

²⁵From you comes my praise in the great congregation;
    my vows I will pay before those who fear him.
²⁶The poor shall eat and be satisfied;
    those who seek him shall praise the LORD.
    May your hearts live forever!

²⁷All the ends of the earth shall remember
    and turn to the LORD;
  and all the families of the nations
    shall worship before him.
²⁸For dominion belongs to the LORD,
    and he rules over the nations.

²⁹To him, indeed, shall all who sleep in the earth bow down;
>   before him shall bow all who go down to the dust,
>   and I shall live for him.

³⁰Posterity will serve him;
>   future generations will be told about the Lord,

³¹and proclaim his deliverance to a people yet unborn,
>   saying that he has done it.

Respond: What a vision of the past, the present and the future! Your kingdom has dawned. You really rule the nations. We see the pledge of your presence that will fill history and take us into Kingdom Come. In joy and celebration we say, "It is finished! You have done it!" Maranatha! Come, Lord Jesus.

SOME FURTHER REFLECTIONS

Psalm 6 is also a lament. You may wish to study it on your own, noting its similarities and differences.

Small Group Study of Psalm 22

The following comments are directed to the leader.

Introduction

Introduce the group to the concept of praying through the psalms by briefly summarizing your own experience of praying Psalm 22. Don't mention any of the details of the psalm itself, its content or its ultimate aim. Just describe the general idea. Then lead the group into the psalm by asking the following questions.

Group Instruction and Questions

1. Have one person read Psalm 22 in its entirety at an ordinary pace.

2. Have another person read it very slowly, with a pause after each verse.

3. A third reading at a normal pace would be appropriate, but you can skip this if it looks as if members of the group are getting restless.

4. What is the main topic of the psalm? Who is the implied voice (speaker) of the psalm? In the New Testament, who quotes the opening verse (Mark 15:34)? Under what circumstances?

5. Summarize the flow of ideas in the psalm. (If this is found difficult, refer to the section on rational structure in this chapter. Then focus on the details by asking the following questions.)

6. There is an abrupt shift in idea and emotion in this psalm. Where does this occur? From the standpoint of the psalmist, what has happened to cause this shift? From the standpoint of Jesus, how is this shift appropriate?

7. What details in the psalm are fulfilled in the Gospel accounts of

the crucifixion? (To answer this question, have each of four persons in the group silently read one of the following Gospel accounts: Mark 15:16-39; Matthew 27:27-54; Luke 23:26-49; John 19:16-37. Have the readers tell what they have found.)

8. How does the fact that Jesus quoted verse 1 from the cross affect our understanding of the psalm?

9. How could David be so depressed as to think himself a worm?

10. Given that Jesus is the incarnate Son of God, how could he think of himself as a worm? (If no one mentions that Jesus might feel this way because he was bearing the burden of our sins, then suggest this: If David or any of us could feel subhuman, would not that misperception be part of our sinful character and thus be borne by Jesus? The point of this question is to help participants understand that the whole psalm could well represent the heart and mind of Jesus on the cross.)

11. According to verses 21b-31, who is to praise God? What, therefore, should be our role today?

Directed Prayer

One way to follow the lead of Psalm 22:21b-31 is to praise God together by praying the entire psalm. The following can serve as a script for such prayer. If members of the group have copies of this book, ask them to put them aside and listen to your instruction.

Leader: Let us pray through Psalm 22. (*You as leader read the psalm and direct the group.*)

> [1]My God, my God, why have you forsaken me?
>> Why are you so far from helping me, from the words of my groaning?

[2]O my God, I cry by day, but you do not answer;
   and by night, but find no rest.

Leader: Lord, we come to you now. The words of David and Jesus, the ancient Hebrews and the church down through the ages are on our lips. Cause us to reflect on what these words meant to them. *(Pause in silence for a few minutes.)*

Now let us reflect on what they mean to us. Pray them for yourself if you are in a similar situation. Pray them for those not in this group whom you know are struggling with their faith. *(Reread verses 1-2. Then pause.)*

[3]Yet you are holy,
   enthroned on the praises of Israel.
[4]In you our ancestors trusted;
   they trusted, and you delivered them.
[5]To you they cried, and were saved;
   in you they trusted, and were not put to shame.

Leader: Reflect on the history of Israel—the exodus especially. Then reflect on Jesus growing up in the care of Mary and Joseph. *(Pause.)*

[6]But I am a worm, and not human;
   scorned by others, and despised by the people.
[7]All who see me mock at me;
   they make mouths at me, they shake their heads;
[8]"Commit your cause to the LORD; let him deliver—
   let him rescue the one in whom he delights!"

Leader: Reflect on how David could think himself subhuman. *(Pause.)* Reflect on how Jesus might have felt like a worm as he bore the burden of your sins on the cross. *(Pause.)*

> [9]Yet it was you who took me from the womb;
>> you kept me safe on my mother's breast.
> [10]On you I was cast from my birth,
>> and since my mother bore me you have been my God.

Leader: Thank God for his care for David, Jesus, and your birth and childhood. *(Pause.)*

> [11]Do not be far from me,
>> for trouble is near
>> and there is no one to help.

Leader: Pray this verse for yourself. *(Reread the verse.)*

> [12]Many bulls encircle me,
>> strong bulls of Bashan surround me;
> [13]they open wide their mouths at me,
>> like a ravening and roaring lion.

> [14]I am poured out like water,
>> and all my bones are out of joint;
> my heart is like wax;
>> it is melted within my breast;
> [15]my mouth is dried up like a potsherd,
>> and my tongue sticks to my jaws;
>> you lay me in the dust of death.

> [16]For dogs are all around me;
>> a company of evildoers encircles me.
> My hands and feet have shriveled;
> [17]I can count all my bones.

They stare and gloat over me;
   ^{18}they divide my clothes among themselves,
      and for my clothing they cast lots.

Leader: As I reread these verses slowly, picture the scene in your mind. Imagine David languishing alone at night, speaking these words to God. *(Reread these verses. Pause.)*

Leader: Again as I reread these verses slowly, picture Jesus on the cross. *(Reread these verses. Pause.)*

   ^{19}But you, O LORD, do not be far away!
      O my help, come quickly to my aid!
   ^{20}Deliver my soul from the sword,
      my life from the power of the dog!
   ^{21}Save me from the mouth of the lion!

Leader: Reflect on the intensity of this plea for God to come. *(Reread these verses. Then pause.)*

      From the horns of the wild oxen you have rescued me.
   ^{22}I will tell of your name to my brothers and sisters;
      in the midst of the congregation I will praise you:
   ^{23}You who fear the LORD, praise him!
      All you offspring of Jacob, glorify him;
      stand in awe of him, all you offspring of Israel!
   ^{24}For he did not despise or abhor
      the affliction of the afflicted;
   he did not hide his face from me,
      but heard when I cried to him.

Leader: Reflect on the radical shift in tone. Think about what has happened to prompt it. Thank God for his dramatic answer to

David's and Jesus' plea. Make your own vow to praise God now—
and over and over—for his delivery of David and Jesus and you!
(*Pause.*)

> [25]From you comes my praise in the great congregation;
>   my vows I will pay before those who fear him.
> [26]The poor shall eat and be satisfied;
>   those who seek him shall praise the LORD.
>   May your hearts live forever!

> [27]All the ends of the earth shall remember
>   and turn to the LORD;
>   and all the families of the nations
>   shall worship before him.
> [28]For dominion belongs to the LORD,
>   and he rules over the nations.

> [29]To him, indeed, shall all who sleep in the earth bow down;
>   before him shall bow all who go down to the dust,
>   and I shall live for him.
> [30]Posterity will serve him;
>   future generations will be told about the Lord,
> [31]and proclaim his deliverance to a people yet unborn,
>   saying that he has done it.

Leader: Praise and thank God for his character of righteousness and
love, for his delivery of David, Israel, Jesus, the church and you.
(*Pause.*)

In joy and celebration we say, "It is finished! You have done it!"
Maranatha! Come, Lord Jesus. Amen.

(*It would be appropriate to end your time together with two hymns: one reflecting Jesus' suffering, such as "O Sacred Head Now Wounded," and another expressing ecstatic and upbeat praise. This will imitate the structure of Psalm 22.)*

Some Parting Remarks

Psalm 6 is another psalm of lament. You might suggest that participants read and study it on their own, comparing and contrasting it with Psalm 22.

2

A KING AND PRIEST FOREVER

Psalm 110

As Christians, we have come to know Jesus as Savior and Lord. We get to know who he is through the New Testament, especially the Gospels, as we see him walk the roads of Israel and speak with a host of different kinds of people—high and low, socially important and outcast. Our understanding is deepened by these encounters with Jesus in Scripture.

But there is more to know about Jesus—some of it quite hard to understand even when we study. Yet if we want to deepen our relationship with God, if we want him to fill the vacuum in our heart, we should learn all we can. In Psalm 110 we get a further glimpse into who Jesus really was, for Jesus used this psalm as a clue to his real identity—not just as a prophet or wise man but as king and priest. It is not easy to grasp the import of this psalm, but it is well worth the work to do so.

As with Psalm 22, Jesus explicitly linked himself with Psalm 110. So do did the early church. And so should we.

Many of us will have come upon Psalm 110 not just while reading the Psalms but also while reading the New Testament. The opening verse, the psalm's most puzzling one, is quoted twice by Jesus (Matthew 22:41-45 and 26:64), twice by the apostle Peter (Acts 2:34-35; 1 Peter 3:22), three times by the apostle Paul (1 Corinthians 15:25; Ephesians 1:20; Colossians 3:1) and twice by the writer of Hebrews (Hebrews 1:13; 10:13). Verse 4 is quoted three times in Hebrews (5:6; 7:17, 21). As Derek Kidner says, Psalm 110 "was destined to form the basis of the apostle's teaching on the exaltation, heavenly session and royal priesthood of Christ. It is one of the most quoted of all the psalms." It may seem odd to identify the psalm as a prayer. "But," as Stanley Jaki says, "pray this psalm we must, and more fervently than any other psalm because Christ hallowed it in a very special sense."

As with all the psalms we are learning to pray, we want to begin with the psalm itself, trying first to absorb the words and flow of the text without explicit reference to Jesus and the New Testament. There will plenty of time to study after we have read well and deeply.

PSALM 110

Assurance of Victory for God's Priest-King
Of David. A Psalm.

> [1]The LORD says to my lord,
>   "Sit at my right hand
> until I make your enemies your footstool."
>
> [2]The LORD sends out from Zion
>   your mighty scepter.
>   Rule in the midst of your foes.
> [3]Your people will offer themselves willingly
>   on the day you lead your forces

on the holy mountains.
From the womb of the morning,
like dew, your youth will come to you.
⁴The LORD has sworn and will not change his mind,
"You are a priest forever according to the order of
Melchizedek."

⁵The Lord is at your right hand;
he will shatter kings on the day of his wrath.
⁶He will execute judgment among the nations,
filling them with corpses;
he will shatter heads
over the wide earth.
⁷He will drink from the stream by the path;
therefore he will lift up his head.

This psalm is difficult to understand. It is all the more important that we read it over and over till we get an inner sense of its flow, though we may not yet have a grasp of its meaning. So give the psalm several more readings—aloud as well as silently.

GETTING AT THE MEANING OF PSALM 110

The first puzzling question we must answer concerns the very first line: Who is speaking to whom? Who is "the LORD" and who is "my lord"? From the text itself, the answer is not obvious. If Jesus himself had not answered the question as he posed the verse as a conundrum to the Pharisees while he was teaching in the temple, we could, I think, take two quite different views.

Since in this book we are interested not only in the original conception of the psalmist but in the place this psalm took in the life, ministry and self-understanding of Jesus, it seems wise to emphasize the way Jesus himself understood the psalm. As Derek Kidner says, "Our Lord gave full weight to David's authorship and David's words, stressing the former twice by the expression 'David himself,' and by the comment that he was speaking 'in the Holy Spirit' (Mk. 12:36f.) and by insisting that his terms presented a challenge to accepted ideas of the Messiah, which must be taken seriously." Peter too stressed the contrast between David and "his lord" (Acts 2:33-35). Perhaps in the final analysis they could be reconciled by seeing in the psalm a first meaning for its original context and a second meaning when interpreted by Jesus, but for a host of reasons (which you can find in a note at the end of this book), I will not do that here. Instead I will take my cue from Jesus' comments in Matthew 22:41-46 and assume that they are as apt for the meaning of the psalm within the Old Testament context as for the meaning of the psalm for Jesus. So let us see what Jesus had to say.

> Now while the Pharisees were gathered together, Jesus asked them this question: "What do you think of the Messiah? Whose son is he?" They said to him, "The son of David." He said to them, "How is it then that David by the Spirit calls him Lord, saying,
>
>   'The Lord said to my Lord,
>   "Sit at my right hand,
>   until I put your enemies under your feet" '?
> If David thus calls him Lord, how can he be his son?" No one was able to give him an answer, nor from that day did anyone dare to ask him any more questions.

What was there in this scholarly puzzle that stopped the Pharisees in their critical tracks? Did they sense that Jesus was claiming to be David's Lord? Certainly the apostles and the early church

would come to view this passage from the Psalms as Jesus' declaration of his unique status before God the Father. Moreover, the
rabbis, who had held that Psalm 110 is messianic, apparently
became troubled by the early Christian reference to this psalm in
defense of the conviction that Jesus was and is the Messiah. In any
case, the first-century rabbis soon ceased considering the psalm
messianic; their successors recovered the notion some four hun-
dred years later.

Jesus identifies the speaker of the psalm as David. Not all psalms
that are designated a "psalm of David" were necessarily written by
David. But if we can trust Jesus, as we surely must, then we need seek
no further for an answer.

So David is the speaker of the first verse. We can now paraphrase
and outline the psalm as follows.

The first oracle: Messiah as King on God's right hand
¹   [David says to Israel, his readers (in the book of Psalms) or lis-
     teners in the temple,] The Lord God (Yahweh) said to the
     my Lord, my King, the Messiah, "Sit at my right hand until
     I make your enemies your footstool."

The King-Messiah proclaimed as ruler and warrior
²   [David now turns to the King-Messiah and says,] The LORD
     (Yahweh) sends out from Zion your mighty scepter. May
     you rule in the midst of your foes!
³   Your people will offer themselves willingly (to be among your
     forces) on the day you lead your forces on the holy moun-
     tains.
     From the womb of the morning, like dew, your youth will be
     restored.

The second oracle: King-Messiah proclaimed as priest forever

4   [David then says to King-Messiah,] The LORD (Yahweh) has sworn and will not change his mind, "You, King-Messiah, are a priest forever according to the order of Melchizedek."

King-Messiah proclaimed as victorious warrior

5   [David turns finally to Yahweh and says,] My Lord (King-Messiah) is at your right hand; he will shatter kings on the day of his wrath.

6   He will join the battle and execute judgment among the nations, filling them with corpses; he will shatter heads over the wide earth.

7   He will drink from the stream by the path and will lift his head high.

I realize that even this attempt to clarify the meaning of the psalm is difficult to understand. So let me try again, this time paraphrasing even further and putting the psalm in prose.

1   King David says to Israel, over whom he rules, that Yahweh spoke these words as he placed David's lord, the longed-for Messiah, on the throne: "Sit at my right hand until I make your enemies your footstool."

2   Then King David addresses his lord as the King-Messiah and says, "Yahweh establishes your reign from Zion [Jerusalem]. Rule, then, in the midst of the foes who surround you.

3   Your people will willingly join your forces as you assemble on the mountains in Israel. You will find your strength renewed like the morning dew.

4   Furthermore, Yahweh has taken an oath that rests on the strength of his character and cannot be broken. Not only

are you, King-Messiah, the king but, Yahweh says, "You are a priest forever in the order of Melchizedek." In other words, your priesthood does not derive from the Levites, who have often broken their vows and been unfaithful, but is in the line of Melchizedek, a priest of Salem [an earlier name for Jerusalem]. Melchizedek is a figure from the past who blessed our great father Abraham [Genesis 14:18-20]. Having appeared in our Scriptures without introduction and exiting without further comment [until New Testament times in Hebrews 5:5-10 and 6:19—7:28], Melchizedek's priesthood is divinely established. Your priesthood, King-Messiah, is forever."

5   David then addresses Yahweh: "My Lord (King-Messiah) is at your right hand; he will shatter kings on the day of his wrath.

6   He will join the battle and execute judgment among the nations, filling them with corpses; he will shatter heads over the wide earth.

7   Successful in battle, he will drink from the stream by the path and will lift his head high in victory."

JESUS AND THE PSALM

How, then, did Jesus understand his relationship to this psalm? The answer to this question has two dimensions.

The first is evident in Jesus' references to Psalm 110 in his polemic against the Pharisees and in his defense before the Sanhedrin. By quoting the psalm (Matthew 22:41-45; Mark 12:35-37 and Luke 20:41-44), he is challenging the religious leaders. He is proposing a puzzle he knows they cannot solve with their own notion of who the Messiah will be. Jesus focuses on the nature of the Messiah as a person closely related to God himself—one who is a king greater than David and an eternal priest of a higher order than the Levites. He is not to be equated, as was the custom of the time, with a political leader who will restore Israel to independence and power. As R. T. France says: "The Messianic dominion was not to be won by his own power, but would be conferred on him by God, and would be exercised in a realm higher than that of national kingship, at the right hand of God. It carried a priestly function, and it would last forever."

The Pharisees thought the psalm was *about* David, not *by* David. But, Jesus asks, how could it be about David? That would mean that the Messiah was both David's lord and David's son. It is a conundrum to which they have no answer.

But there is another dimension. What role did Psalm 110 have in Jesus' own self-understanding? Jesus alludes to the psalm in Matthew 26:64 (Mark 14:62 and Luke 22:69). A casual reader may miss this allusion, but scholars easily detect it. The situation is this. On the night he is betrayed, Jesus is hauled before the high priest, who puts him "under oath before the living God" (Matthew 26:63) and says, "Tell us if you are the Messiah, the Son of God." Jesus replies:

You have said so. But I tell you,

From now on you will see the Son of Man
seated at the right hand of Power
and coming on the clouds of heaven. (Matthew 26:64)

Jesus' answer is yes, but with a qualification. Yes, he is the Messiah, but not in the sense that the high priest is expecting—one who by force will restore Israel to political independence from Rome. Rather, he is the Messiah who is to be equated with the one who sits on the right hand of God (Psalm 110:1) and the Son of Man (Daniel 7:13-

14), a transcendent figure who in Daniel's vision comes "with the clouds of heaven" and is given an everlasting kingship over all nations.

How did Jesus come to have this self-understanding? We must be somewhat speculative at this point. We cannot get inside Jesus' head any more than we can get inside the head of anyone but ourselves. But if the premise of this book is basically correct, Jesus learned much about who he was from his deep engagement with the Hebrew Scriptures. Given this, it is easy to see how his self-understanding might have developed. Psalm 110 was considered messianic by those by whom he would have been taught as a boy and young man.

Imagine him coming across this psalm in his study or meditation. A profound depth of meaning leaps from the two revelations about the king who is being enthroned. What does the psalm mean? He asks his teachers. They put it this way: "Yahweh says to young David, 'I declare you an exalted king, almost equal to me in glory. You will win many battles. You will be forever young. You will also be a priest forever in an order far higher than that of the Levites.' "

This puzzles him. It doesn't seem to fit the David who walks the pages of the Scriptures. Was David a priest? he asks his teacher. His teacher waffles. Then as Jesus' grasp of the Scriptures matures, his conception of Messiah becomes richer; he begins to see a complex pattern emerge. Prophet, priest, king, suffering servant, Son of Man, Messiah begin to come together in his mind. Gradually he comes to see himself as the one sent to fulfill all these roles. Psalm 110, he concludes is not about David; it is about the king who is also the Messiah.

As he matures further, he associates himself with John the Baptist and his message. When he is baptized, heaven is opened and "the Holy Spirit descended upon him in bodily form like a dove. And a voice came from heaven, 'You are my Son, the Beloved' " (Luke 3:21). Then comes his time in the wilderness, when Satan tempts him to violate his sense of calling (Luke 4:1-13). He quiets Satan with his deep knowledge of Scripture and soon after begins acting out his calling, tying his mission to that of Isaiah and performing the deeds called for by Isaiah 61:1-2 (Luke 4:18-19).

In the midst of his ministry, Jesus asks Peter who people think he is and affirms Peter's own inspired view that Jesus is the Messiah. However, he corrects Peter's notion that the Messiah can't suffer and die (Mark 8:31-33). Later still he takes Peter, James and John aside privately, is transfigured before them, and talks with Elijah and Moses, who suddenly appear alongside him. A voice from a cloud that overshadows them says, "This is my Son, the Beloved; listen to him!" (Mark 9:7).

However long it has been since Jesus understood who he was, there can be no doubt now. Jesus came to see himself as the Messiah, the one who would come to deliver Israel and the whole world from the powers of evil. He would be the one to inaugurate the kingdom of God. But note: this would be on his terms and the terms of Scripture rightly understood, not in the terms of the religious leaders. As R. T. France says, "Jesus never mentioned the term *Messiah* without contrasting his own concept with that of others of his day."

By the time he posed the conundrum of Psalm 110:1 to the Pharisees, Jesus was well versed in both who he was and how the Scriptures prefigured his life. And as we saw in the chapter on Psalm 22, he could take a psalm and make it his own in a way impossible for any ancient psalmist or any of us today.

DAVID AND THE PSALM

If Psalm 110 is, as I have argued, truly a psalm of David, then how did he pray his own prayer? What was his relation to what he had written? Again, there will be some speculation here, but some things seem reasonable to assume or conclude from reflective and studied reading.

David has been inspired by the Holy Spirit, says Jesus (Matthew 22:43). He has been given two oracles from Yahweh himself. We could ask how these oracles came to him, but we cannot find an answer. As far as we can know, he somehow became conscious that God had spoken and he had heard. What God told him was something that he could never have known apart from being told. This is what revelation is—a word from another, a word that carries only the authority of the other who has spoken. In this case, it is a word that cannot possibly be anything but true. The second oracle emphasizes this when David says, "The LORD has sworn and will not change his mind" (Psalm 110:4).

In the case of both oracles, David may have been told things he did not well understand. He does seem, however, to understand some things, for he immediately says that his lord (whom we know now as Messiah-King) will rule and the people will willingly follow, as his lord is victorious and his lord's youth blossoms. With such a prophetic vision, David could, and surely did, rejoice. Praise to Yahweh would naturally flow. Though we don't see that explicitly in the psalm, the psalm itself is a paean of praise.

David's reaction to the second oracle is itself a bit puzzling. Verses 5-7 do not seem to reflect the announced priesthood of David's lord. They make no comment on Melchizedek or his priestly class, leaving this oracle to be understood, if at all, only by reference to Genesis 14:18. Verses 5-7 rather expand on the kingly role announced in verse 1. Again we can see them as implicit praise of Yahweh and David's lord.

Did David prostrate himself before the ark as he prayed this psalm? Was he so humbled by these oracles that he lay there in silence? Did he think about these words as he ruled Israel, taking confidence that though he might fail in his endeavors, there was one coming who would fulfill the role not only of king of Israel but of Savior of the world? We can only speculate. But such speculation at least gives us a hint of what *we* might do as we pray the psalm.

THE EARLY CHURCH AND THE PSALM

Peter, Paul and the writer of Hebrews all quote or allude to Psalm 110.

Peter. In his sermon at Pentecost, the apostle Peter cites verse 1 and asserts that Jesus' resurrection and ascension show that God "has made [Jesus] both Lord and Messiah" (Acts 2:34-36). And in his first letter he again cites that verse, saying Jesus "has gone into heaven and is at the right hand of God, with angels, authorities, and powers made subject to him" (1 Peter 3:22). The emphasis is on the exaltation of Jesus as the incarnate and transcendent Lord (King) Messiah.

Paul. The apostle Paul alludes to verse 1 when he explains how Christ is the first of many who will be resurrected. When "the end" comes, the Messiah will triumph over all God's enemies: "For he must reign until he has put all his enemies under his feet" (1 Corinthians 15:25; see also Ephesians 1:20 and Colossians 3:1).

Hebrews. The writer of the Hebrews quotes verse 1 twice (1:13; 10:13) and verse 4 three times (5:6; 7:17, 21). Hebrews 1:13 takes Jesus' view of verse 1, emphasizing that Jesus has a greater status than that of the angels; and Hebrews 10:12-13 declares that the first half of verse 1 is already fulfilled but that the second half's fulfillment, as was indicated by the apostle Paul, will come later: "When Christ had offered for all time a single sacrifice for sins, 'he sat down at the right hand of God,' and since then has been waiting 'until his enemies would be made a footstool for his feet.' "

Psalm 110:4, however, gets much more attention in Hebrews. Hebrews 4:14—5:7 and 7:1-28 are long discourses on the priesthood of Jesus, explaining why Jesus' priesthood is of a higher order—the order of Melchizedek—than the Levite priesthood of Aaron. If it were not for this discourse, I rather imagine that no modern scholar could begin to understand what Psalm 110:4 is all about.

OUR RELATION TO THE PSALM

How, then, do we relate to the psalm? Is there any way we can pray a psalm that at first blush has so little to do with us? How can Jaki say, "But pray this psalm we must, and more fervently than any other psalm because Christ hallowed it in a very special sense"? Surely our prayer will be different from those of other psalms. For we are neither David to whom the revelation came nor Jesus who claimed to fulfill the revelation.

But we should not so easily accept the notion that the psalm has no relation to us. First, we are, or can and should be, the people of God. That means that we can offer ourselves willingly on the day King-Messiah leads his "forces on the holy mountains." We may not know just what this means, but we can offer ourselves every day and that way we will not miss the day of King-Messiah's victory. Second, we can join David in the implicit praise the psalm raises. And we can add to the psalm the perspective given us by Jesus and the apostles in two ways. We can see Jesus in the psalm, and we can pray the psalm in light of that perception. That is what we will try to do in the following personal liturgy.

PRAYING PSALM 110

Reread the psalm aloud slowly; then pray it section by section.

¹The LORD says to my lord,
  "Sit at my right hand
  until I make your enemies your footstool."

Respond: Lord, I want to pray this psalm even though I find it mysterious and difficult. Thank you for the word from Jesus and the explanations from the scholars.

You have revealed to the great King David a great mystery. You have shown him a glimpse of your complex character, perhaps even a hint of your nature as Trinity. When I see the psalm as Jesus saw it, the true King-Messiah comes into focus. Thank you, Lord, for this revelation, this insight into your sovereignty! Hallelujah!

Indeed, I repeat the words of David:

¹The LORD says to my lord,
  "Sit at my right hand
  until I make your enemies your footstool."

Pause now in silence. Then continue.

²The LORD sends out from Zion
  your mighty scepter.
  Rule in the midst of your foes.

Respond: I picture a mighty king standing tall with a massed army behind him. To this warrior-king flock even more. The apostles teach that this is a vision of Jesus the King-Messiah returning at the end of the age. *Pause in silence to let this vision sink in. Don't try to make a theology out of this picture. Just let it persist as an image.*

³Your people will offer themselves willingly
  on the day you lead your forces
  on the holy mountains.

From the womb of the morning,
> like dew, your youth will come to you.

Respond: There strides King-Messiah Jesus—powerful, triumphant, youthful with the bloom of spring. Glorious and resplendent. *Pause in silence to let this picture sink deep into your conscious mind. Then continue.*

> [4]The LORD has sworn and will not change his mind,
>> "You are a priest forever according to the order
>> of Melchizedek."

Respond: The priesthood of Melchizedek. What a strange notion! King-Messiah is the priest of an order that seems to have no beginning and no end. It is not limited by the failures of the Hebrew people and their priests. King-Messiah is priest forever, forever mediating between us and the holy God. Hallelujah! *Pause in silence.*

> [5]The Lord is at your right hand;
>> he will shatter kings on the day of his wrath.
> [6]He will execute judgment among the nations,
>> filling them with corpses;
> he will shatter heads
>> over the wide earth.
> [7]He will drink from the stream by the path;
>> therefore he will lift up his head.

Respond: Picture this second vision in your mind. Let it settle in. Then close your prayer: Lord, these visions are too much for me to understand. They still seem foreign. They portend more than I can comprehend. And that is part of what leads me to pray this psalm. I want to stand with David and see what he saw. And I want to stand under Jesus to understand what he understood. It is too much for me. But what I grasp is enough. In Jesus Christ, the incarnate Son of God, you have fulfilled the oracles given to David. Now fulfill the visions. Even so come, Lord Jesus!

SOME FURTHER REFLECTIONS

Why not select this psalm for reading and praying during your daily devotions for one or two weeks? That will help you overcome some of its mystery without diminishing its power or the power of the Lord.

Small Group Study of Psalm 110
The following comments are directed to the leader.

Introduction

I don't think there is any way around saying that this psalm may prove more difficult than most for a group to understand. As leader, you will probably have to supply more information, more perspective, than you would usually need to provide. The members of the group will, I think, not mind this, for without some information that is not available to most readers today, the psalm would remain a proverbial black box—awesome but utterly mute.

Group Instruction and Questions

1. Have one person read Psalm 110 at an ordinary pace.

2. Have a second person read the psalm slowly, pausing briefly after each verse.

3. Have another person reread the psalm at an ordinary pace.

4. What verses in the psalm stand out as especially odd, important or strange? Why? When participants have answered, close off the conversation by asking the next question.

5. In verse 1, who do you think is "the LORD"? Who is "my lord"? Who is the "my" of "my lord"? (These will probably cause a lot of confused discussion. So ask the next question.)

6. Twice Jesus referred to this verse. (Have someone read Matthew 22:41-45.) How did Jesus answer the questions asked in question 5?

7. Have someone read Matthew 26:64. What light do Jesus' comments throw on the identity of "my lord" in Psalm 110:1?

8. What characteristics of "my lord" do Psalm 110:2-3 and 5-7 reveal? When do you think the events described have occurred or will occur? What does Hebrews 10:13 say about the timing?

9. What characteristic of "my lord" is added in verse 4? Who was Melchizedek (Genesis 14:18)? (Here you will need to supply information from the discussion earlier in this chapter.)

10. At this point or before, you may wish to give each participant a photocopy of the prose paraphrase found on pp. 53-54 above. You have permission from the publisher to do this. Pause in your discussion to let each person read it silently. Then have one read it aloud. Try to get each participant (or most of them) to understand the basic flow and meaning of the psalm.

11. Ask someone to summarize the discussion and explain why this psalm, as unlike any others as it is, is still an important one to pray. Then proceed to the following liturgy.

Directed Prayer

The following script may help the group to pray the psalm.

Leader: Because this psalm is filled with images, I will ask you to imagine several scenes. Make your imagination a part of your prayer. Let us pray Psalm 110 together.

> ^{1}The LORD says to my lord,
>   "Sit at my right hand
> until I make your enemies your footstool."

Leader: Recall that this is David saying this to the one who will later be revealed as Jesus, the Messiah. I repeat. (*Read verse 1 again.*) In your mind's eye, imagine this conversation going on in the heavens.

(Reread verse 1 and continue with verses 2-3.)

> ²The LORD sends out from Zion
>> your mighty scepter.
>> Rule in the midst of your foes.
> ³Your people will offer themselves willingly
>> on the day you lead your forces
>> on the holy mountains.
> From the womb of the morning,
>> like dew, your youth will come to you.

Leader: Picture this scene in your mind. *(Reread verses 2-3; then pause.)* Consider your relationship to Jesus Christ. Are you among his people? Do you answer his call when he asks you to do something or be someone? Reflect on your relationship with this commanding figure and tell him how you feel about being under his charge. Thank him for his salvation and the fact that you stand with him and not among his enemies. *(Pause.)*

> ⁴The LORD has sworn and will not change his mind,
>> "You are a priest forever according to the order
>>> of Melchizedek."

Leader: Lord Jesus, we confess that we don't know much about the priesthood of Melchizedek, but we know that you are not only king but priest as well, one who lays our sins before God. You not only carry them there but bear their burden. You who knew no sin became sin for us that we might become the righteousness of God. We praise you. *(Pause.)*

> ⁵The Lord is at your right hand;
>> he will shatter kings on the day of his wrath.

⁶He will execute judgment among the nations,
　　filling them with corpses;
　he will shatter heads
　　over the wide earth.
⁷He will drink from the stream by the path;
　　therefore he will lift up his head.

Leader: Picture this in your mind. *(Reread verses 5-7 slowly, then pause.)* We lift up our minds, our hearts, our selves to you. Take us, use us in the establishment of your kingdom. Reign over our lives. And in your good time, come, Lord Jesus. Wind up history and reign forever. Amen.

Some Further Reflections

Encourage participants to study the book of Hebrews, where some of the mystery of Jesus as priest will become less mysterious.

3

THE STONE THE BUILDERS REJECTED

Psalm 118

Sometimes to us Jesus is an enigmatic figure. He says things that seem just too radical. "Love your enemies," he said; "do good to those who despise you." This seems impossible. Then he says, "Pluck out your eye if what you see leads you into sin." This seems crazy. Where does he get off saying these things? Who is he, anyway? The religious leaders of his day had the same reaction. But to them what Jesus said was worse than impossible or crazy. They thought he was undermining their authority. He even spoke of destroying the temple.

No wonder that near the end of his ministry these leaders challenged him: "By what authority are you saying the things you do? They are very disturbing. We don't like them. They're revolutionary."

In his answer Jesus chose a verse from the middle of Psalm 118 and lifted its meaning for ancient Israel into a prophecy of his own time. Later his disciples extended that prophecy and related it to the formation of the church. The verse itself is a bit of a puzzle, of course, and so is its setting in Psalm 118. We will consider the setting first, then examine the brilliant jewel that sparkles from its setting.

The setting, Psalm 118, is a liturgy. We need to understand what that means. Our churches today take at least two distinct views of the role of liturgy in worship. Liturgical churches such as the Catholic, Lutheran and Episcopal opt for the traditional view that the sacraments are more than "mere" allegories with no participation in the reality they symbolize. They see the transcendent as profoundly interacting with the immanent: Christ is present in the bread and wine. Nonliturgical churches such as Baptist, Pentecostal and Evangelical Free are children of the Reformer Ulrich Zwingli. They claim that participating in the rituals and liturgy of the Lord's Supper merely draws a picture of the atonement. To put it crassly, nothing spiritual is happening; only a "story," albeit one packed with spiritual significance, is being reenacted.

Christian readers today come to the Bible with one or the other of these views. Whichever view they hold is usually so deeply embedded in their psyche that they are unaware of it. It just seems natural that rituals and liturgies are either vehicles mediating spiritual reality or allegories merely signifying this reality. This situation is illuminated by the sorts of understandings that are likely to emerge when readers approach Psalm 118, one of the psalms most pregnant with meaning for both its Hebrew participants and its Christian readers.

PSALMS AS LITURGIES

Christians worshiping in liturgical churches do not have to be told that the psalms are well fit for their worship. Quotations from the psalms, even whole psalms, are read by both the worship leader and the congregation, often in antiphony. Yet some of the psalms are so liturgical that while the meaning of their parts seems clear, they don't have an obvious unified rational structure. Frankly, they come off as puzzles, brilliant quilt squares that when sewn together just don't make sense.

Psalm 118 is one such psalm. It contains several winners in the memory department. These verses lie just below the surface of our conscious mind and emerge like the lines of music we sometime just can't get out of our head. Watch for them as you read the psalm. But after several readings, try to notice not only these memorable lines but also some of the places where the speaker seems to change and where something seems to be going on around those who are speaking the lines.

PSALM 118

A Song of Victory

¹O give thanks to the LORD, for he is good;
   his steadfast love endures forever!

²Let Israel say,
   "His steadfast love endures forever."
³Let the house of Aaron say,
   "His steadfast love endures forever."
⁴Let those who fear the LORD say,
   "His steadfast love endures forever."

⁵Out of my distress I called on the LORD;
   the LORD answered me and set me in a broad place.
⁶With the LORD on my side I do not fear.
   What can mortals do to me?
⁷The LORD is on my side to help me;
   I shall look in triumph on those who hate me.
⁸It is better to take refuge in the LORD

than to put confidence in mortals.
⁹It is better to take refuge in the LORD
    than to put confidence in princes.

¹⁰All nations surrounded me;
    in the name of the LORD I cut them off!
¹¹They surrounded me, surrounded me on every side;
    in the name of the LORD I cut them off!
¹²They surrounded me like bees;
    they blazed like a fire of thorns;
    in the name of the LORD I cut them off!
¹³I was pushed hard, so that I was falling,
    but the LORD helped me.
¹⁴The LORD is my strength and my might;
    he has become my salvation.

¹⁵There are glad songs of victory in the tents of the righteous:
  "The right hand of the LORD does valiantly;
¹⁶   the right hand of the LORD is exalted;
    the right hand of the LORD does valiantly."
¹⁷I shall not die, but I shall live,
    and recount the deeds of the LORD.
¹⁸The LORD has punished me severely,
    but he did not give me over to death.

¹⁹Open to me the gates of righteousness,
    that I may enter through them
    and give thanks to the LORD.

²⁰This is the gate of the LORD;
    the righteous shall enter through it.

²¹I thank you that you have answered me
    and have become my salvation.
²²The stone that the builders rejected
    has become the chief cornerstone.
²³This is the LORD's doing;
    it is marvelous in our eyes.
²⁴This is the day that the LORD has made;
    let us rejoice and be glad in it.
²⁵Save us, we beseech you, O LORD!
    O LORD, we beseech you, give us success!

²⁶Blessed is the one who comes in the name of the LORD.
    We bless you from the house of the LORD.
²⁷The LORD is God,
    and he has given us light.
  Bind the festal procession with branches,
    up to the horns of the altar.

²⁸You are my God, and I will give thanks to you;
    you are my God, I will extol you.

²⁹O give thanks to the LORD, for he is good,
    for his steadfast love endures forever.

GETTING AT THE MEANING OF PSALM 118

After spending some time reading and rereading, what impressed you? What lines jumped out? The first and last? Or what about "Blessed is the one who comes in the name of the LORD" (v. 26)? Or the one that has supplied the title to this chapter (v. 22)? One of my favorites, perhaps because I like vivid poetry, is this one:

¹²They surrounded me like bees;

they blazed like a fire of thorns;
  in the name of the LORD I cut them off!

Another is this:

²⁴This is the day that the LORD has made;
  let us rejoice and be glad in it.

It used to ring in my mind as I walked to work each morning.

Liturgical Structure

But can one easily make sense of the structure of the psalm? Not, I think, without digging in and seeing the psalm as a liturgy used in a national religious ceremony, quite possibly at Passover. One way to open the entire psalm to the light is to see the liturgical structure something like this:

The scene is a procession starting somewhere outside the gates of the temple. Along the way to the temple, these lines are spoken.

LECTOR (AS WORSHIP LEADER):
  ¹Give thanks to the LORD, for he is good;
    his steadfast love endures forever!

ISRAEL (HALF THE CELEBRANTS):
  ²[Let Israel say,]
    "His steadfast love endures forever."

HOUSE OF AARON (REMAINING CELEBRANTS):
  ³[Let the house of Aaron say,]
    "His steadfast love endures forever."

ALL CELEBRANTS:
  ⁴[Let those who fear the LORD say,]

"His steadfast love endures forever."

LECTOR (AS VOICE OF THE KING/ISRAEL):
[5]Out of my distress I called on the LORD;
    the LORD answered me and set me in a broad place.
[6]With the LORD on my side I do not fear.
    What can mortals do to me?
[7]The LORD is on my side to help me;
    I shall look in triumph on those who hate me.
[8]It is better to take refuge in the LORD
    than to put confidence in mortals.
[9]It is better to take refuge in the LORD
    than to put confidence in princes.

[10]All nations surrounded me;
    in the name of the LORD I cut them off!
[11]They surrounded me, surrounded me on every side;
    in the name of the LORD I cut them off!
[12]They surrounded me like bees;
    they blazed like a fire of thorns;
    in the name of the LORD I cut them off!
[13]I was pushed hard, so that I was falling,
    but the LORD helped me.
[14]The LORD is my strength and my might;
    he has become my salvation.

[The celebrants pause in their march to the temple for congregational singing. The lector is still speaking.]

[15]There are glad songs of victory in the tents of the righteous:

[Then the celebrants sing.]

ALL CELEBRANTS:

> "The right hand of the LORD does valiantly;
> ¹⁶ the right hand of the LORD is exalted;
>   the right hand of the LORD does valiantly."

LECTOR (AS VOICE OF THE KING):

> ¹⁷I shall not die, but I shall live,
>   and recount the deeds of the LORD.
> ¹⁸The LORD has punished me severely,
>   but he did not give me over to death.

[The celebrants arrive outside the gate of the temple. The lector cries out.]

> ¹⁹Open to me the gates of righteousness,
>   that I may enter through them
>   and give thanks to the LORD.

GATEKEEPERS:

> ²⁰This is the gate of the LORD;
>   the righteous shall enter through it.

LECTOR (AS VOICE OF THE KING/ISRAEL):

> ²¹I thank you that you have answered me
>   and have become my salvation.

[The lector pauses here to signal that a prophetic word is about to be spoken—an oracle bearing the authority of Yahweh himself.]

> ²²The stone that the builders rejected
>   has become the chief cornerstone.

[The lector then takes a different stance and tone of voice to reflect on the oracle.]

> ²³This is the LORD's doing;
>   it is marvelous in our eyes.

²⁴This is the day that the LORD has made;
>   let us rejoice and be glad in it.

²⁵Save us, we beseech you, O LORD!
>   O LORD, we beseech you, give us success!

²⁶Blessed is the one who comes in the name of the LORD.
>   We bless you from the house of the LORD.

²⁷The LORD is God,
>   and he has given us light.

[The lector turns to the temple priests.]

LECTOR (AS VOICE OF THE KING TO THE TEMPLE PRIESTS):
>   Bind the festal procession with branches,
>   up to the horns of the altar.

[The lector turns to the altar.]

LECTOR (AS VOICE OF THE KING/ISRAEL/CELEBRANTS):
>   ²⁸You are my God, and I will give thanks to you;
>   you are my God, I will extol you.

[The lector finally turns to the celebrants.]

LECTOR (AS VOICE OF THE KING TO THE CELEBRANTS):
>   ²⁹O give thanks to the LORD, for he is good,
>   for his steadfast love endures forever.

The One Voice of the King, the Many Voices of Ancient Israel

This liturgical layout should go a long way toward clarifying the psalm as it was used and understood in ancient Israel.

As a ritual enacted at Passover, the psalm reminded the Israelites of their relationship to Yahweh and the power by which the king would be successful. They would see the king leading Israel into ritual participation in the reign of Yahweh. Beginning and ending with the call to give thanks to God for his eternal love, the stirring voice of the king would recount and give Yahweh credit for his own successes, and the people would sing a mighty hymn of praise to Yahweh. Arriving at the temple gate and being led by the king into the temple, they would be thrilled to hear an oracle they could readily understand. After all of Israel's rejections in Egypt and Palestine, they would ritually enact the truth that God was in charge after all and that the king who represented them would be the foundation stone for a new era.

For ancient Israel, in other words, "the stone that the builders rejected" was both their king and their nation. No wonder they could joyfully proclaim:

> [29]O give thanks to the LORD, for he is good,
>   for his steadfast love endures forever.

The Voice of Jesus

Now shift the scene to Jesus teaching in the temple courts. Three Gospels tell the same story (Matthew 21:23-46; Mark 11:27—12:12; Luke 20:1-19). As Matthew puts it, the "chief priests and the elders of the people" were troubled by the words and works of Jesus. They challenged him: "By what authority are you doing these things, and who gave you this authority?" (Matthew 21:23).

Jesus made a threefold response: (1) he asked them by whose authority John the Baptist performed baptisms, (2) he told a parable of two sons, one who said he would obey their father and didn't and the other who said he wouldn't obey and did, and (3) he told a parable of wicked tenants who kill the son of the vineyard's owner. Each of these responses was a stinging rebuke to those who challenged him, and they knew it. But he was not finished. He drew the moral of the final parable with a flourish:

Jesus said to them, "Have you never read in the scriptures:

'The stone that the builders rejected
    has become the cornerstone;
this was the Lord's doing,
    and it is amazing in our eyes'?

Therefore I tell you, the kingdom of God will be taken away from you and given to a people that produces the fruits of the kingdom. The one who falls on this stone will be broken to pieces; and it will crush anyone on whom it falls." (Matthew 21:42-44)

Jesus saw himself as the rejected stone that would be the foundation of the new temple, the one finally to realize the kingdom of God. He saw those who rejected him crushed by this stone. The scene is rife with irony. In the next few days his fall (crucifixion) would crush the ones who had rejected him. In his death and resurrection was the salvation of all who would accept him.

We should look too at verse 26. All four Gospels recount Jesus' entrance into Jerusalem (Matthew 21:9; 23:39; Mark 11:9; Luke 19:38; John 12:13). This event had, of course, taken place not long before the confrontation just discussed. The crowds cried,

Hosanna to the Son of David!
    Blessed is the one who comes in the name of the Lord!
(Matthew 21:9)

Jesus willingly accepted their praise. And soon afterward, as he lamented over Jerusalem, he reiterated: "I tell you, you will not see me again until you say, 'Blessed is the one who comes in the name of the Lord' " (Matthew 23:39).

These two references to Psalm 118 were enough already to assure his rejection by the religious leaders.

The Perspective of the Early Church

Early in the life of the church, religious leaders in Jerusalem wanted to know where the disciples got their authority to teach that Jesus was resurrected from the dead. The apostle Peter cited Psalm 118:22:

> This Jesus is
> "the stone that was rejected by you, the builders;
>   it has become the cornerstone." (Acts 4:11)

Much later in his ministry, he expanded on the metaphor:

> Come to him [Christ], a living stone, though rejected by mortals yet chosen and precious in God's sight, and like living stones, let yourselves be built into a spiritual house, to be a holy priesthood, to offer spiritual sacrifices acceptable to God through Jesus Christ. For it stands in scripture:
>
> "See, I am laying in Zion a stone
>   a cornerstone chosen and precious;
> and whoever believes in him
>   will not be put to shame" [quoting Isaiah 28:16].
>
> To you then who believe, he is precious; but for those who do not believe,
>
> "The stone that the builders rejected
>   has become the very head of the corner,"

and

"A stone that makes them stumble,
> and a rock that makes them fall" [quoting Isaiah 8:14].
(1 Peter 2:4-8)

Peter here extends the stone image so that Jesus forms the corner-stone of the new temple, that is, the church. Thus an image begun in ancient Israel was extended in significance from Israel to Jesus to the early church, suggesting that further extension to the church of our day is justified. Much in the psalms that is fulfilled in Jesus and his time receives a further fulfillment in ours and in the age to come.

The Psalm for Us

How then shall we understand this liturgical psalm? In the Christian tradition we do not have a ready-made rite in which we enact this ceremony. There is no temple toward which to process. This does not stop us, however, from seeing in our mind's eye what the Israelites did. Nor does it keep us from using, as did Jesus and the early church, elements of the psalm in our private and public worship. Before suggesting a private and public liturgy for us, however, I want to make several points.

First, the psalm itself and Jesus' own reference to it are a piece of an apologetic for Jesus as the Christ, the one whom Israel longed for and the one to whom we give our utmost allegiance. It helps confirm that Jesus thought of himself as more than one in a long line of prophets. He was a liar, a lunatic with visions of grandeur, or the Lord himself.

Second, we can—and on Palm Sunday often do—reenact the entrance of Jesus into Jerusalem, knowing that this ritual reflects a rite that remembers not only Jesus but also the ancient kings of Israel.

Third, if our church is liturgical, we can be reminded that ritual is not just dead repetition but live participation in the embodied meaning of the ancient Jewish and Christian faith.

Fourth, if our church is nonliturgical, we can learn to appreciate the richness of a tradition that, though foreign to our experience, is justified by the Psalms.

With these in mind, let us pray the psalm.

PRAYING PSALM 118

Read the entire psalm aloud slowly; then pray it section by section.

> [1]O give thanks to the LORD, for he is good;
>> his steadfast love endures forever!
> [2]Let Israel say,
>> "His steadfast love endures forever."
> [3]Let the house of Aaron say,
>> "His steadfast love endures forever."
> [4]Let those who fear the LORD say,
>> "His steadfast love endures forever."

Respond: Lord, I hear the command to give you thanks, and I do so for your goodness, for your steadfast love that endures forever. I see the ancient Israelites lined up in ranks speaking this line, and I rejoice that these words can also be my own: Your steadfast love endures forever. *Pause and reflect on verses 1-4.*

> [5]Out of my distress I called on the LORD;
>> the LORD answered me and set me in a broad place.
> [6]With the LORD on my side I do not fear.
>> What can mortals do to me?
> [7]The LORD is on my side to help me;
>> I shall look in triumph on those who hate me.

[8]It is better to take refuge in the LORD
    than to put confidence in mortals.
[9]It is better to take refuge in the LORD
    than to put confidence in princes.

Respond: I know, Lord, that here the king, or at least his spokesperson, is speaking these lines. But some of them fit my experience. *Pause to cite an instance or two and thank God for relieving your distress.* May the wisdom of the king stay with me as I keep my ultimate confidence in you and not in my government or any human institution.

[10]All nations surrounded me;
    in the name of the LORD I cut them off!
[11]They surrounded me, surrounded me on every side;
    in the name of the LORD I cut them off!
[12]They surrounded me like bees;
    they blazed like a fire of thorns;
    in the name of the LORD I cut them off!
[13]I was pushed hard, so that I was falling,
    but the LORD helped me.
[14]The LORD is my strength and my might;
    he has become my salvation.

Respond: Take a few moments to picture the images in these lines, the bees, the blazing thorns, the pushing hard and falling, the cutting off of his enemies. Lord, the king has been strengthened by your might. May you strengthen me to fend off the evils that beset me. *Pause and name some of these.*

[15]There are glad songs of victory in the tents of the righteous:
    "The right hand of the LORD does valiantly;

16   the right hand of the LORD is exalted;
         the right hand of the LORD does valiantly."

Respond: I see a huge chorus singing and praising God for his victory over evil.

17I shall not die, but I shall live,
         and recount the deeds of the LORD.

Respond: The king has great confidence in you, Lord. He recounts the deeds that have brought victory to his nation and to himself. May I too live for your glory!

18The LORD has punished me severely,
         but he did not give me over to death.

Respond: The king has undergone just retribution for his sins, but you have preserved him. Is there here a hint of the Suffering Servant? You punished Christ for the sins of the world, but he conquered death. The grave could not hold him. Hallelujah! *Pause to consider these verses as fulfilled in Christ.*

19Open to me the gates of righteousness,
         that I may enter through them
         and give thanks to the LORD.

Respond: Open the gates of righteousness to me too!

20This is the gate of the LORD;
         the righteous shall enter through it.

Respond: I know only the righteous shall enter. But I come in righteousness under the blood of Christ. I want to live in your temple. I want to sense your presence and respond with praise and thanksgiving. I know the condition for living in your courts, Lord. I do not measure up. But I also know that by your grace I can enter the temple where you are ever present. I can live and move and have my being in you.

>   [21]I thank you that you have answered me
>   and have become my salvation.

Respond: Thank you! Thank you! Thank you! *Pause to reinforce the seriousness of what you have just said.*

>   [22]The stone that the builders rejected
>   has become the chief cornerstone.

Respond: Glory to you, Lord Jesus Christ! Glory to you, the rejected one who has become the cornerstone of the new temple!

>   [23]This is the LORD's doing;
>   it is marvelous in our eyes.

Respond: This is your doing. It is marvelous in all our congregations' eyes!

>   [24]This is the day that the LORD has made;
>   let us rejoice and be glad in it.

Respond: And what a day it is! *Pause to let the glory of this day of Yahweh, this day of the Lord Jesus Christ, this day of the Holy Spirit sink below your conscious mind.*

>   [25]Save us, we beseech you, O LORD!
>   O LORD, we beseech you, give us success!

Respond: May every day now be a day of your success in my life and the life of my community.

^{26}Blessed is the one who comes in the name of the LORD.
    We bless you from the house of the LORD.

Respond: I bless and thank and glorify you!

^{27}The LORD is God,
    and he has given us light.

Respond: You, Lord God, are my light and my salvation.

    Bind the festal procession with branches,
        up to the horns of the altar.

Respond: I see the people bringing their sacrifices or their symbols before the altar of the temple. May I bring to you my self and lay it on your altar in worship! *Pause for several moments.*

^{28}You are my God, and I will give thanks to you;
    you are my God, I will extol you.

Respond: Reread this verse as your own prayer. Then read the following verse as a closing vow to call others to thank the Lord.

^{29}O give thanks to the LORD, for he is good,
    for his steadfast love endures forever.

Respond: Amen.

SOME FURTHER REFLECTIONS

As I first drafted this liturgy, I was suddenly brought up short. I had forgotten for a moment that verses 20-26 were not my own but belonged to an Israelite king (or perhaps a priest) centuries ago. They fit my soul to a T. Verse 23 has been a part of my psyche for many years, for which I give thanks. The blessed day that the Lord Jesus entered his Jerusalem, the day he gave his life for my (our) transgressions, the day he rose from the dead, the day he comes again, the day his victory is complete—these and all days are *the day* the Lord has made. Let us rejoice and be glad in it!

Small Group Study of Psalm 118
The following comments are directed to the leader.

Introduction

I recommend that you spread out your group study over two sessions. In the first session lead the group into discovering the various speakers of the liturgy and the progress of the pilgrims. Close with a prayer relating to what you have discovered and discussed.

Do not fear to be creative in leading this study. One of the goals is to help participants get a sense of the ritual that lies behind the liturgy. Ideas acted out serve to prompt learning and stimulate memory.

Group Instruction and Questions for Session 1

1. Have one person read Psalm 118 at an ordinary pace.

2. Have a second person read the psalm slowly, pausing briefly after each verse.

3. Have another person reread the psalm at an ordinary pace.

4. What lines in this psalm stick out as familiar or especially memorable? Why? (Take a number of answers, but do not let the conversation go on too long.)

5. Despite these vivid lines, did any of you find this psalm confusing? Explain. (When participants have expressed what will probably be some frustration, proceed by helping them see the psalm as a liturgy. Ask such questions as, Who seems to be speaking in these verses [name them]? Take the group through the psalm until the speakers have been identified and the ritual action understood. You may use the liturgy on pp. 73-76, and you have the publisher's permission to photocopy it for each participant. But I recommend that this be distributed after the group, with your

help, has reached its own conclusions. If time remains, select readers for each of the voices—lector/king, Israel, house of Aaron, gatekeepers, priests. Then read through the liturgy a couple of times to get the sense of its flow. Clarify any confusion that might still remain.)

6. Close the study with your own prayer, based on themes you have noted in the psalm.

Group Instruction for Session 2

1. Have one person read Psalm 118 at an ordinary pace.

2. If you did not do this during the first session, distribute the liturgy to the participants, choose readers for the various speakers in the psalm, and reenact the psalm.

3. By this time it should be clear that the central focus of the psalm is the oracle in verse 22. What makes it so striking? How did Jesus interpret the verse? (Assign individual participants to read for themselves one of three passages: Matthew 21:23-44; Mark 12:1-12; Luke 20:8-19. Then have them report their findings.)

4. According to Jesus, who is the stone? In the view of ancient Israel, how does the stone function? How will it function in the time of Jesus?

5. Why is verse 26 so familiar to many of us who grew up in a church? (This is an easy question to answer. But have one person read Mark 11:8-10 for the answer.) What made the verse so relevant to Jesus' entry into Jerusalem? (He was enacting the entrance of the king to the city of the temple; later he would enter and teach at the temple, causing all sorts of protest and eventually triggering his own arrest.)

6. What added significance does verse 26 have in light of how Jesus again refers to it in Matthew 23:29?

7. How did Peter interpret Psalm 118:22? (See Acts 4:11 and 1 Peter 2:4-8.) What implications does Peter's interpretation have for us? That is, how is Jesus the cornerstone in our day?

When you feel that the group is ready for corporate prayer, you may use the liturgy below.

Directed Prayer

The following script may help the group to pray the psalm.

Leader: Let us pray Psalm 118 together.

> ¹O give thanks to the LORD, for he is good;
>   his steadfast love endures forever!

Leader: Picture the various groups responding to the lector:

> ²Let Israel say,
>   "His steadfast love endures forever."
> ³Let the house of Aaron say,
>   "His steadfast love endures forever."
> ⁴Let those who fear the LORD say,
>   "His steadfast love endures forever."

Leader: Lord, we hear ranks upon ranks of the ancient Hebrews proclaim: "Your steadfast love endures forever." And we rejoice. *(Pause.)*

> ⁵Out of my distress I called on the LORD;
>   the LORD answered me and set me in a broad place.
> ⁶With the LORD on my side I do not fear.

What can mortals do to me?
[7]The LORD is on my side to help me;
   I shall look in triumph on those who hate me.
[8]It is better to take refuge in the LORD
   than to put confidence in mortals.
[9]It is better to take refuge in the LORD
   than to put confidence in princes.

Leader: Lord, these words of the king fit us too. Think now of an instance or two of distress, and thank God for relieving it. *(Pause.)* May the wisdom of the king stay with us! May we keep our ultimate confidence in you and not in any government or any human institution.

[10]All nations surrounded me;
   in the name of the LORD I cut them off!
[11]They surrounded me, surrounded me on every side;
   in the name of the LORD I cut them off!
[12]They surrounded me like bees;
   they blazed like a fire of thorns;
   in the name of the LORD I cut them off!
[13]I was pushed hard, so that I was falling,
   but the LORD helped me.
[14]The LORD is my strength and my might;
   he has become my salvation.

Leader: Take a few moments to picture the images in these lines—the bees, the blazing thorns, the pushing hard and falling, the cutting off of his enemies. *(Pause.)* Lord, the king has been strengthened by your might. May you strengthen us to fend off the evils that beset us. As we pause, think of some of these that fit you. *(Pause.)*

¹⁵There are glad songs of victory in the tents of the righteous:
    "The right hand of the LORD does valiantly;
 ¹⁶   the right hand of the LORD is exalted;
    the right hand of the LORD does valiantly."

Leader: Picture a huge chorus—all the Hebrew celebrants—singing and praising God for his victory over evil. *(Pause.)* Now hear the king say,

¹⁷I shall not die, but I shall live,
    and recount the deeds of the LORD.

Leader: The king has great confidence in you, Lord. He recounted the deeds that brought victory to his nation and to himself. So we, too, are living. May we live for your glory!

¹⁸The LORD has punished me severely,
    but he did not give me over to death.

Leader: The king has undergone just retribution for his sins, but you have preserved him. Is there a hint here of the Suffering Servant? You punished Christ for the sins of the world, but he conquered death. The grave could not hold him. Hallelujah! *(Pause.)* We now pray for ourselves the words of this psalm.

¹⁹Open to me the gates of righteousness,
    that I may enter through them
    and give thanks to the LORD.

Leader: Yes, open to us the gates of righteousness!

²⁰This is the gate of the LORD;
    the righteous shall enter through it.

Leader: Lord, only the righteous shall enter. But we come in righteousness under the blood of Christ. We want to live in your temple. We want to sense your presence and respond with praise and thanksgiving. We know the condition for living in your courts, Lord. We do not measure up. But by your grace we can enter the temple where you are ever present. We can live and move and have our being in you.

²¹I thank you that you have answered me
>   and have become my salvation.

Leader: Thank you! Thank you! Thank you! (*Pause, then continue with the great oracle to follow.*)

²²The stone that the builders rejected
>   has become the chief cornerstone.

Leader: Suddenly these words drop precipitously from our lips. Where do they come from ? Not out of the blue, but from you, Lord God. Glory to you, Lord Jesus Christ! Glory to you, the rejected one who has become the cornerstone of the new temple! These words are not just about rejected Israel; they are about you!

²³This is the LORD's doing;
>   it is marvelous in our eyes.

Leader: Indeed this is your doing. And it is marvelous in all our eyes!

²⁴This is the day that the LORD has made;
>   let us rejoice and be glad in it.

Leader: And what a day it is! As I pause, let's allow the glory of this day of Yahweh, this day of the Lord Jesus Christ, this day of the Holy Spirit to sink below our conscious mind. Hallelujah! (*Pause.*)

[25]Save us, we beseech you, O LORD!
> O LORD, we beseech you, give us success!

Leader: May every day now be a day of success in our lives!

[26]Blessed is the one who comes in the name of the LORD.
> We bless you from the house of the LORD.

Leader: We bless and thank and glorify you!

[27]The LORD is God,
> and he has given us light.

Leader: You, Lord God, are our light and our salvation.

> Bind the festal procession with branches,
>> up to the horns of the altar.

Leader: We have all but forgotten for the moment that this psalm was first for those Israelites of old. We are now drawn back to that scene. See the people bringing their sacrifices and ritual symbols before the altar of the temple. May each of us bring his or her self and lay it before your altar in worship! *(Pause for several moments.)*

[28]You are my God, and I will give thanks to you;
> you are my God, I will extol you.

Leader: Those words are now the words of each of us. We vow to heed your call.

[29]O give thanks to the LORD, for he is good,
> for his steadfast love endures forever.

All: Amen.

Parting Remarks

These will have been two long studies and prayers. Why not just end your session quickly, bid each other goodbye and promise to pray for each other? More seriously, why not come to realize that prayer is often work? Work, yes, but the wages received for that work are eternal joy.

4

YOU ARE MY SON

Psalm 2

Imagine Jesus worshiping in the synagogue as a teen-age boy. Out of the liturgy, perhaps sung, perhaps spoken, comes this decree to the king of Israel:

"You are my son; today I have begotten you."

How would this dramatic oracle strike him? Of course, we can't answer that question with any certainty, but we can easily see why the early church found this psalm profoundly messianic.

So far the psalms we have studied and prayed are those that the New Testament explicitly tells us were psalms that Jesus himself had internalized and applied to his ministry and self-understanding. But there are others that the early church quickly saw as receiving their ultimate fulfilment in him. Perhaps chief among them is Psalm 2. It is quoted by the congregation of early believers (Acts 4:25-26), the apostle Paul (Acts 13:33), five times by the apostle John (Revelation 2:26-27; 6:15; 11:15 and 18; 19:15) and twice by the writer of Hebrews (Hebrews 1:5 and 5:5).

Let us, then, pay special attention to the psalm, first for as much as we can absorb by multiple readings apart from the scholarship and then from a close look at what the church both early and late has to say.

Psalm 2

God's Promise to His Anointed

[1]Why do the nations conspire,
   and the peoples plot in vain?
[2]The kings of the earth set themselves,
   and the rulers take counsel together,
   against the LORD and his anointed, saying,
[3]"Let us burst their bonds asunder,
   and cast their cords from us."

[4]He who sits in the heavens laughs;
   the LORD has them in derision.
[5]Then he will speak to them in his wrath,
   and terrify them in his fury, saying,
[6]"I have set my king on Zion, my holy hill."

[7]I will tell of the decree of the LORD:
 He said to me, "You are my son;
   today I have begotten you.
[8]Ask of me, and I will make the nations your heritage,
   and the ends of the earth your possession.
[9]You shall break them with a rod of iron,
   and dash them in pieces like a potter's vessel."

[10]Now therefore, O kings, be wise;
   be warned, O rulers of the earth.

¹¹Serve the LORD with fear,
    with trembling ¹²kiss his feet,
  or he will be angry, and you will perish in the way;
    for his wrath is quickly kindled.

    Happy are all who take refuge in him.

GETTING AT THE MEANING OF PSALM 2

Certainly on the surface Psalm 2 is not difficult to understand. It begins dramatically with the astonished psalmist suddenly expostulating: Why do the nations think they can overthrow the king of Israel? Don't they know better? It moves to the mocking words of Yahweh, who declares that Yahweh, having appointed his son as king of Israel, has everything under his control. The kings of the surrounding nations had better recognize this and submit to Yahweh. It will be best for them and for all who trust Yahweh.

Rational Structure

In the following outline we can easily see the pattern.

Astonishment at the presumption of the kings of the nations (why do they conspire against God?), verses 1-3

The response of Yahweh (the enthronement of Israel's king), verses 4-6

Yahweh's declaration (the king is my son), verses 7-9

Warning to the kings of the nations (God in anger may annihilate you), verses 10-12a

Final encouraging counsel to all (those who take refuge in God will be happy), verse 12b

Cast your mind back over the text and the sequence of ideas until you grasp the psalm's basic intellectual flow.

Emotional Structure

Psalm 2 is nothing if not emotional. It is a roller coaster that begins with arrogance, irony, mockery and stern foreboding and yet ends with happiness. God is not to be tampered with by mere kings of the nations, no matter how exalted they think they are. But God rewards those who fear and honor him. Here is a chart of the emotional flow.

verses 1-3	Astonishment at the arrogance of foreign kings
verse 4	Mocking laughter of Yahweh
verses 5-6	Anger of Yahweh
verses 7-9	Confident acceptance of God's decree
verse 10	Warning of God's wrath
verses 11-12a	Fear, trembling and sense of submission
verse 12b	Prospect of happiness

Reread the psalm several times, focusing on this emotional flow and its connection to the ideas presented.

PSALM 2 IN THE HISTORY OF ISRAEL

We have no difficulty in identifying Psalm 2 as an "enthronement psalm," that is, a composition used as part of the coronation ceremony of Israel's kings. The text is generic, applicable to any king in David's line; so its origin cannot be precisely dated. There are many such "royal psalms," and we will have cause later in this book to consider another of them, Psalm 45. Interestingly, neither Psalm 2 nor any of the others is explicitly messianic; that is, none of them points explicitly to a future figure who will be "concerned with the final redemption" of his children.

Primarily the royal psalms celebrate the king of Israel as a "son of God," not by any means a divine figure—that would be blasphemy—but one who relates to Yahweh as a son to his father and as one "anointed" for the task of ruling Israel with justice and mercy and protecting Israel from foreign invaders. The king is called to be the king among kings, the one whom others, if they know what's good for them, should acknowledge and honor. As we can see, Psalm 2 has all these features.

The fact that the royal psalms were not originally considered messianic, however, does not mean that they have no messianic dimension, only that it was not made explicit until Jesus and the early church began to see them in that light. For one thing, no actual king of Israel was able to fully embody the exalted role to which he was called. If David or his successors ever prayed Psalm 2:8-9, God chose not to answer that prayer as it appears to require:

> [8]Ask of me, and I will make the nations your heritage,
>   and the ends of the earth your possession.
> [9]You shall break them with a rod of iron,
>   and dash them in pieces like a potter's vessel.

The kingdom of God was not yet inaugurated as it would be by Jesus. "Everything foretold in the enthronement psalms about the foundation of God's kingdom we see fulfilled in Jesus," Pius Drijvers says. So we now turn to consider that fulfillment.

JESUS, THE EARLY CHURCH AND THE ROYAL PSALMS

We have already seen that Jesus understood Psalm 110 in terms of his own identity and mission. But while Jesus himself does not refer to Psalm 2, a host of his followers have. Moreover, I think we can be confident that as he was meditating and studying the Scriptures, Jesus would have come to see even more in the Psalms than his followers did. The kings of Israel were enthroned. They were to rule with justice and mercy. Mostly they did not do that. The reign of David and his descendants was to extend around the world. Even if that meant only the then "known world," that had not occurred. The reign was to have been, if not eternal, at least perpetual. But it hadn't been, and even now, with the puppet-king Herod on the throne and Israel under the military thumb of Rome, something was dreadfully awry.

Would not Jesus have seen this? As he came to understand his various roles as prophet, priest, king and Suffering Servant, would he not read these royal psalms as requiring both a present and a future fulfillment—the first to bear the sins of Israel and the whole world and thus complete their salvation from the power of sin through his death and resurrection, and the second to come again to realize the kingdom of God by delivering his people from the presence of evil and its consequences? There is, of course, some speculation in this scenario, but it is surely consistent with how the early church understood the royal psalms as it worshiped.

Peter. In an early gathering of new believers, the whole congregation is said to have "raised their voices together" to praise God for delivering the apostles Peter and John from the grasp of the religious authorities. They began by acknowledging God as sovereign Lord and creator. Then they declared that it was "by the Holy Spirit through our ancestor David, your servant," that God said,

> Why did the Gentiles rage,
>   and the peoples imagine vain things?

The kings of the earth took their stand,
and the rulers have gathered together
against the Lord and against his Messiah. (Acts 4:25-26)

They see these verses as being fulfilled by Jesus' and their own persecution by the Romans and their fellow Jews.

Paul. In Antioch of Persidia, the apostle Paul proclaimed to the Jews who lived there that Jesus was the son of David whom the Jews in Jerusalem had killed but who had then been resurrected. "You are my Son; today I have begotten you," Paul quoted from Psalm 2; he then added two short sections from Isaiah 55:3 and Psalm 116 (see Acts 13:33-35). His point was that Jesus was the one who has come to redeem Israel. But the Jews rejected that message, and as a result, Paul turned to the Gentiles as the main focus of his witness.

John. In the letter to Thyatira in Revelation, God encourages the church to stay faithful: "To everyone who conquers and continues to do my works to the end," he says,

I will give authority over the nations;
to rule them with an iron rod, as when clay pots are
shattered. (Revelation 2:26-27)

Here, then, the role of the king is given to the followers of Jesus.

Perhaps the most dramatic citations in Revelation come in the apostle's great vision. The seventh trumpet sounds and loud voices from heaven say:

The kingdom of the world has become the kingdom of our Lord
and of his Messiah. (Revelation 11:15)

Soon after this, "the twenty-four elders who sit on the thrones" say:

The nations raged,
>   but your wrath has come,
>   and the time for judging the dead,
> for rewarding your servants, the prophets
>   and saints and all who fear your name,
>   both small and great,
> and for destroying those who destroy the earth.
> (Revelation 11:18)

Finally when a rider on a white horse (a symbol for the victorious Christ) appears, there comes from his mouth "a sharp sword with which to strike down the nations, and he will rule them with a rod of iron" (Revelation 19:15). Given this family of citations, it is clear that John had absorbed Psalm 2, as some of its details are fulfilled in this vision of God's judgment.

Hebrews. The writer of the Hebrews cites the psalm, first, to show Jesus' superiority over the angels:

> For to which of the angels did God ever say,
>   "You are my Son;
>   today I have begotten you"? (Hebrews 1:5)

Then he combines that verse from Psalm 2 with one from Psalm 110 to show that Jesus was appointed by God to be both son and priest:

> So also Christ did not glorify himself in becoming a high priest, but was appointed by the one who said to him,
>
>   "You are my Son,
>   today I have begotten you";
>
> as he says also in another place,

> "You are a priest forever,
>> according to the order of Melchizedek." (Hebrews 5:5-6)

The early church clearly saw Psalm 2 as being fulfilled by Jesus not only in his earthly life but by his return in glory, when all of history will be wrapped up in becoming the kingdom of God.

OUR RELATION TO THE PSALM

How then shall we read and pray the psalm? To take it merely as an ancient song of Israel and adapt it to our current situations would be to truncate its implications in both our typically religious life and our typically secular life. Let us live with Psalm 2, drawing from it both what the ancient Israelites drew (that God was in charge and appointed kings in Israel to rule wisely and justly, though they failed) and what the early church understood (that the fulfillment of ancient Israel's hope is bound up with ours and is yet to be made manifest). In light of that, let us pray.

PRAYING PSALM 2

Read the entire psalm aloud slowly; then pray it section by section.

> ¹Why do the nations conspire,
>> and the peoples plot in vain?
> ²The kings of the earth set themselves,
>> and the rulers take counsel together,
>> against the LORD and his anointed, saying,
> ³"Let us burst their bonds asunder,
>> and cast their cords from us."

Respond: Help me, Lord, as I pray this psalm, to enter into its ethos, to feel the astonishment of the psalmist as he considers the plots of ancient Israel's enemies. *Reread verses 1-3 slowly, envisioning the counsels of Israel's enemies. Pause. Think of Jesus as he contemplated these verses. What might he have seen as his and his nation's enemies? What kinds of plots was he suffering at different stages of his life?* Lord Jesus, King of kings and Lord of lords, hear my prayer as I try to imagine your mindset as you prayed this psalm. And let me realize that your enemies have yet to be vanquished here in this world. May their plots come to nothing!

> [4]He who sits in the heavens laughs;
>   the LORD has them in derision.
> [5]Then he will speak to them in his wrath,
>   and terrify them in his fury, saying,
> [6]"I have set my king on Zion, my holy hill."

Respond: Father God, I see you in my mind's eye, laughing at the foolish presumption of those who oppose your rule, not only in ancient Israel and the time of the Roman occupation but even now, as pundits proclaim the machinations of their own minds and secular intellectuals declare that they can live life as fulfilled atheists. Keep my Christian friends and me from attributing our grasp of your goodness, glory and righteous judgment to the superiority of our unaided minds. We receive from you whatever grasp of truth we have. Thank you for setting your King in Zion, for bringing the Messiah to Israel, for putting yourself on the throne of my heart. May he reign there forever!

> [7]I will tell of the decree of the LORD:
>   He said to me, "You are my son;
>   today I have begotten you.
> [8]Ask of me, and I will make the nations your heritage,

and the ends of the earth your possession.
⁹You shall break them with a rod of iron,
   and dash them in pieces like a potter's vessel."

Respond: Thank you, Yahweh, Father-God, for declaring the sonship of your kings and especially the sonship of Jesus. Jesus the Christ realized his sonship in all he did while here on earth, but many people failed to recognize who he was. For my part, I have not been quick to take up my share of the role you have given my Christian community to work for the coming of your kingdom. I know King Jesus will complete the judgment that David foresaw but couldn't complete. Let justice roll down!

¹⁰Now therefore, O kings, be wise;
   be warned, O rulers of the earth.
¹¹Serve the LORD with fear,
   with trembling ¹²kiss his feet,
  or he will be angry, and you will perish in the way;
   for his wrath is quickly kindled.

Respond: You have warned the kings. You have warned me. May I honor you! And may you reward me not for what I have done but for taking refuge in you! For I know this:

Happy are all who take refuge in him.

Respond: Happy *are* all who take refuge in you! Amen.

Small Group Study of Psalm 2
The following comments are directed to the leader.

Introduction

With Psalm 2 you will be helping participants see that texts of Scripture that are not specifically prayers can provide rich stimulus to learn who God is and to respond to that growing knowledge with prayers that engage the soul at the root of its being.

Group Instruction and Questions

1. Have one person read Psalm 2 at an ordinary pace.

2. Have a second person read the psalm slowly, pausing briefly after each verse.

3. Have another person reread the psalm at an ordinary pace.

4. What part do you think this psalm played in the life of ancient Israel? (If no one catches on that this psalm involves the coronation of a king, you may need to explain that. See pp. 98-99.) What comfort or hope would it give to Israel?

5. What is the overall flow of ideas? What emotions are tied to those ideas? What is the progress of these emotions? That is, on what emotional plane does it begin? Where does it end? (This question will take some time and discussion to answer. Wrap up the discussion by having someone summarize the psalm in a casual paraphrase. Something like the summary on p. 98 will suffice.)

6. The New Testament does not record any times Jesus may have referred to this psalm, yet the early church repeatedly linked him to it. Why? (After several have suggested answers, assign each of the following passages to one or more participants: Acts 4:25-26; Revelation 2:26-27; 6:15; 11:15-18; Hebrews 1:5; 5:5-6. Then

have each explain what he or she has discovered. If this proves too difficult, you may wish to summarize the material on pp. 99-103.)

7. Given what we can see of Israel's use of the psalm and that of the early church, how do you think Jesus understood it? (This is a speculative question. Don't dwell on it too long.)

8. What does the early church's use of the psalm suggest about how we might apply it to our understanding and our liturgies? (Take several answers from participants. Then note that one way to answer this question will be taken up by the guided prayer to follow.)

When you feel that the group is ready for corporate prayer, you may use the following liturgy.

Directed Prayer

The following script may help the group to pray the psalm.

Leader: Let us pray Psalm 2 together.

> [1]Why do the nations conspire,
>   and the peoples plot in vain?
> [2]The kings of the earth set themselves,
>   and the rulers take counsel together,
>   against the LORD and his anointed, saying,
> [3]"Let us burst their bonds asunder,
>   and cast their cords from us."

Leader: Help us, Lord, as we begin to pray this psalm. We want to enter into its ethos, to feel the astonishment of the psalmist as he considers the plots of ancient Israel's enemies. As I reread verses 1-3 slowly, envision the counsels of Israel's enemies. (*Read verses 1-3 again. Pause.*) Think of Jesus as he contemplated these verses. What or whom might he have seen as his and his nation's enemies? (*Pause.*)

What kinds of plots was he suffering at different stages of his life? In the wilderness with Satan? (*Pause.*) With the Pharisees? (*Pause.*) In the Garden of Gethsemane? (*Pause.*) On the cross? (*Pause.*) Lord, let us realize that your enemies have yet to be vanquished here in this world. May their plots come to nothing! (*Short pause.*)

> ⁴He who sits in the heavens laughs;
>> the LORD has them in derision.
> ⁵Then he will speak to them in his wrath,
>> and terrify them in his fury, saying,
> ⁶"I have set my king on Zion, my holy hill."

Leader: Father God, we see you in our mind's eye, laughing at the foolish presumption of those who oppose your rule in ancient Israel (*pause*) . . . at the time of Christ (*pause*) . . . and even now, as pundits proclaim the machinations of their own minds and secular intellectuals declare that they can live life as fulfilled atheists. It is frightening to see your judgment, but we recognize its justice. Let us not attribute our grasp of your goodness, glory and righteous judgment to the superiority of our unaided minds. We receive from you whatever grasp of truth we have. Thank you for setting your king in Zion, for bringing the Messiah to Israel, for putting yourself on the throne of our own hearts. May you reign there forever! (*Short pause.*)

> ⁷I will tell of the decree of the LORD:
>> He said to me, "You are my son;
>> today I have begotten you.
> ⁸Ask of me, and I will make the nations your heritage,
>> and the ends of the earth your possession.
> ⁹You shall break them with a rod of iron,
>> and dash them in pieces like a potter's vessel."

Leader: Thank you, Yahweh, Father God, for declaring the sonship of your kings and especially the sonship of Jesus. Jesus the Christ realized his sonship in all he did while here on earth, but many of the people did not recognize who he was. We ourselves have been slow to take up our share of the work you have given our community to do for the coming of your kingdom. For that we ask your forgiveness.

Now, friends, think of the roles to which we have been called as individuals and as a community. *(Pause.)* We know King Jesus will complete the judgment that David foresaw but couldn't complete. Let justice roll down!

> [10]Now therefore, O kings, be wise;
>> be warned, O rulers of the earth.
> [11]Serve the LORD with fear,
>> with trembling [12]kiss his feet,
> or he will be angry, and you will perish in the way;
>> for his wrath is quickly kindled.

Leader: We hear the warning you gave the kings of the nations and of ancient Israel. You have warned us. May we honor you! And may you reward us not for what we have done but for taking refuge in you. For we know this:

> Happy are all who take refuge in him.

Leader: Happy *are* all who take refuge in you! Amen.

Some Parting Remarks

Encourage group members to return to this psalm with some regularity, at least until it becomes a part of their inner soul. You may also wish to recommend that they study and pray several other "royal psalms," such as 45; 72; 93; 96; 97; 99 and 132. We have already prayed Psalm 110 and will pray Psalm 45.

5

ZEAL FOR YOUR HOUSE

Psalm 69

Troubled? Discouraged? Depressed? Sunk so low you feel you will never find release? Consumed with zeal for the Lord but crushed by rejection from those you thought were your friends? Angry at them? So angry you explode with verbal retaliation? Then this is a psalm for you. And perhaps surprisingly, it was a psalm for Jesus.

Psalm 69 is much quoted in the New Testament, though only once by Jesus. It occurs in close connection with what he was doing, what was happening around him and how others were reacting to him. Moreover, like Psalm 22, much of Psalm 69 may be seen as happening *in* Jesus as he hung on the cross.

But we must not skip the first step in our praying the psalms of Jesus. We must begin with the psalm itself. To enter into the mind of Jesus and to purify our own thoughts, we must participate in the words he read and internalized. Do so now several times before proceeding.

PSALM 69

Prayer for Deliverance from Persecution
To the leader: according to Lilies. Of David.

¹Save me, O God,
    for the waters have come up to my neck.
²I sink in deep mire,
    where there is no foothold;
I have come into deep waters,
    and the flood sweeps over me.
³I am weary with my crying;
    my throat is parched.
My eyes grow dim
    with waiting for my God.

⁴More in number than the hairs of my head
    are those who hate me without cause;
many are those who would destroy me,
    my enemies who accuse me falsely.
What I did not steal
    must I now restore?
⁵O God, you know my folly;
    the wrongs I have done are not hidden from you.

⁶Do not let those who hope in you be put to shame because of me,
    O Lord GOD of hosts;
do not let those who seek you be dishonored because of me,
    O God of Israel.
⁷It is for your sake that I have borne reproach,
    that shame has covered my face.
⁸I have become a stranger to my kindred,

an alien to my mother's children.

[9]It is zeal for your house that has consumed me;
    the insults of those who insult you have fallen on me.
[10]When I humbled my soul with fasting,
    they insulted me for doing so.
[11]When I made sackcloth my clothing,
    I became a byword to them.
[12]I am the subject of gossip for those who sit in the gate,
    and the drunkards make songs about me.

[13]But as for me, my prayer is to you, O LORD.
    At an acceptable time, O God,
    in the abundance of your steadfast love, answer me.
  With your faithful help [14]rescue me
    from sinking in the mire;
  let me be delivered from my enemies
    and from the deep waters.
[15]Do not let the flood sweep over me,
    or the deep swallow me up,
    or the Pit close its mouth over me.

[16]Answer me, O LORD, for your steadfast love is good;
    according to your abundant mercy, turn to me.
[17]Do not hide your face from your servant,
    for I am in distress—make haste to answer me.
[18]Draw near to me, redeem me,
    set me free because of my enemies.

[19]You know the insults I receive,
    and my shame and dishonor;
    my foes are all known to you.

²⁰Insults have broken my heart,
>so that I am in despair.
>I looked for pity, but there was none;
>and for comforters, but I found none.
²¹They gave me poison for food,
>and for my thirst they gave me vinegar to drink.

²²Let their table be a trap for them,
>a snare for their allies.
²³Let their eyes be darkened so that they cannot see,
>and make their loins tremble continually.
²⁴Pour out your indignation upon them,
>and let your burning anger overtake them.
²⁵May their camp be a desolation;
>let no one live in their tents.
²⁶For they persecute those whom you have struck down,
>and those whom you have wounded, they attack still more.
²⁷Add guilt to their guilt;
>may they have no acquittal from you.
²⁸Let them be blotted out of the book of the living;
>let them not be enrolled among the righteous.
²⁹But I am lowly and in pain;
>let your salvation, O God, protect me.

³⁰I will praise the name of God with a song;
>I will magnify him with thanksgiving.
³¹This will please the LORD more than an ox
>or a bull with horns and hoofs.
³²Let the oppressed see it and be glad;
>you who seek God, let your hearts revive.
³³For the LORD hears the needy,

and does not despise his own that are in bonds.

³⁴Let heaven and earth praise him,
the seas and everything that moves in them.
³⁵For God will save Zion
and rebuild the cities of Judah;
and his servants shall live there and possess it;
³⁶   the children of his servants shall inherit it,
and those who love his name shall live in it.

GETTING AT THE MEANING OF PSALM 69

This is a much longer psalm than we have studied so far in this book. But not to worry: it is also one of the easiest to grasp. Its structure is straightforward, its meaning clear. Read it over and over to sink it deep into your conscious and subconscious mind. Then consider both its rational and emotional structure.

Rational and Emotional Structure

	RATIONAL		EMOTIONAL
1	Prayer 1	For deliverance	Desperation
2-5	Lament 1	So many enemies	
2a			Fear
2d			Despair
3			Physical weariness
4			Frustration
5			Puzzled sense of guilt
6	Prayer 2	For God's people	Compassion
7-12	Lament 2	Zeal for God and its results	
7			Shame

	RATIONAL		EMOTIONAL
8			Estrangement
9			Zeal
10-12			Discouragement
13-18	Prayer 3	For deliverance	Desperate hope
19-21	Lament 3	Insults of the enemy	
19			Shame
20			Heartbreak
21			Rising anger
22-28	Cry for vengeance		
22			Vindictiveness
23-28			Full-blown anger
29	Lament 4 and prayer	For deliverance	Gasping hope
30-33	Personal praise	For deliverance	
30a			Rising praise
30b-31			Thankfulness
32-33			Overflowing joy
34-36	Cosmic praise	For the kingdom's coming	Cosmic ecstasy

This psalm has a straightforward flow of ideas, primarily back and forth between four laments and four prayers for protection and deliverance; these are once broken up by a sustained cry for vengeance and then closed off by praise for answered prayer. Review this structure till it becomes clear and obvious to you.

Do you see how the structure of Psalm 69 parallels the structure of Psalm 22? Lament and prayer ebb and flow in verses 1-29. Then there is a sudden shift. Verses 30-36 take on a radically different tone. Something has happened offstage. The psalmist's problem has been solved. His praise, again as in Psalm 22, is both personal and corporate, present and eschatological. It begins with his own time and projects the future. At the very beginning of the *already*—the nation of Israel as a harbinger of the kingdom of God—the psalmist projects a vision of the *not yet*. The sweep of the psalm is cosmic, as is the coming kingdom of God.

The emotional structure is also worth isolating, for it not only parallels the rational structure but strikes us deeply. The range of emotions in such a short poem is staggering. The psalm begins in despair, deepens into frustration and anger, shows occasional glimpses of hope, but near the end blazes up into burning anger and utter vindictiveness. Then, without preparation of any kind, the psalm becomes a paean of praise ending in a sort of cosmic ecstasy. What can account for this but something that happens offstage? We must assume an epiphany, what the Greeks would call a "coming of the gods," or as the Hebrews might put it, the invisible appearance of God himself bringing salvation and complete joy.

How does the psalm accomplish all of this? Let's look at some of the details.

Vivid Images

This is a psalm of vivid images and powerful metaphors. It may seem odd to encourage you to *savor* them, because so many depict the agony of the psalmist—water that comes up to the neck, deep mire, no foothold, deep waters, flood, crying, parched throat, dim eyes. And that's just in the first three verses! But savor them we must if we are to participate aesthetically and spiritually in the predicament of the psalmist. So read the first three verses again. Then read verses 13-15, focusing on the images and the emotions they convey. Scholars say that while this is a psalm "of David," it is not possible to specify precisely what events lie behind the psalm. The lack of specificity, however, means that readers of all eras can easily find corollaries in their own experience to help them participate in these sections of the psalm.

A third section, verses 21-28, is likewise filled with powerful images. This time, however, we will be even less eager to savor them. The psalmist curses his enemies in some of the most unsavory images in the Psalms. We will take up this subject when we look at Jesus' relation to the psalm.

The Prayers Within the Prayer

As we have seen, there are four petition prayers within Psalm 69. Three of them (v. l, vv. 13-18 and v. 29) are requests for deliverance of the psalmist from his enemies. But one, a request for his community, arises out of a brief reflection on the possibility of his own moral culpability. While he objects to being falsely accused of stealing and of having to return what he hasn't taken, he admits that he too may be guilty before God. He says,

> Many are those who would destroy me,
> > my enemies who accuse me falsely.
> What I did not steal
> > must I now restore?
> [5]O God, you know my folly;
> > the wrongs I have done are not hidden from you.

Then he prays for those who may be suffering for sins he is accused of committing.

> [6]Do not let those who hope in you be put to shame because of me,
> > O Lord GOD of hosts;
> do not let those who seek you be dishonored because of me,
> > O God of Israel.

Here, if only for a moment, the psalmist broadens his concern to his community. His personal lament becomes corporate. As we have noted, of course, the conclusion picks up this corporate note and extends it into the future yet to come even for us.

JESUS IN THE PSALM AND THE PSALM IN JESUS

This is a "psalm of David." While it is not necessary to hold that he actually wrote the psalm, it is necessary to accept it as written either for him or about him. In the liturgy we will assume the voice is that of David. But there is another voice as well.

"From start to finish," Michael Wilcock says, Psalm 22 "could have been uttered by [Jesus], with truth and passion, at Calvary. It is not quite the same with 69. Jesus could not, for example, have spoken of his folly and guilt, as verse 5 does—but a similar wealth of quotations and allusions shows how the early church regarded our present psalm." I would add that neither do verses 22-28 reflect Jesus' attitude toward those who crucified him (Luke 23:34), but we will consider this below.

Early in his ministry, according to the Gospel of John, Jesus at the time of the Passover went to the temple and "found people selling cattle, sheep, and doves and the money changers seated at their tables." Angered at the way the temple had been turned into a marketplace, he made a whip of cords and drove them—humans and beasts alike—out. His disciples then remembered that "it was written, 'Zeal for your house will consume me,' " quoting of course the first half of Psalm 69:9 (John 2:13-22).

The second half of verse 9 is quoted by the apostle Paul. He does so to show that as the insults meant for God fell on David, so the insults meant for God fell on Jesus. Even Christ "did not please himself." This shows, Paul says, that "whatever was written in former days was written for our instruction" (Romans 15:3-4). Is this not what we are learning in our study and our psalmic prayer?

Late in his ministry Jesus himself alluded to Psalm 69:4. He warned his disciples at the Last Supper that the "world" would hate them just as it hated him. The world had seen Jesus' deeds and should have accepted him and his ministry. "But now they have seen and hated both me and my Father. It was to fulfill the word that is written in their law, 'They hated me without a cause' " (John 15:24-25). Jesus here associates himself with the agony of the psalmist, claiming to fulfill in himself the words of Scripture.

Psalm 69, however, also prefigures one of the details of the crucifixion mentioned by three of the Gospel writers. Here is John's account of the fulfillment of Psalm 69:21: "After [his putting his mother in John's care], when Jesus knew that all was now finished, he said (in order to fulfill the scripture), 'I am thirsty.' A jar full of sour wine was standing there. So they put a sponge full of the wine on a branch of hyssop and held it to his mouth. When Jesus had received the wine, he said, 'It is finished' " (John 19:28-30).

Matthew places a similar detail earlier in the crucifixion and specifies wine mixed with gall: "When they came to a place called Golgotha (which means Place of a Skull), they offered him wine to drink, mixed with gall; but when he tasted it, he would not drink it" (Matthew 27:33-34). Then Matthew adds a second account that corresponds with the timing in the Gospel of John. Just before his death, Jesus cried out, "My God, my God, why have you forsaken me?" (Matthew 27:46). In Aramaic this sounded like he was calling out for Elijah: "At once one of them ran and got a sponge, filled it with sour wine, put it on a stick, and gave it to him to drink. But the others said, 'Wait, let us see whether Elijah will come to save him' " (Matthew 27:48-49). But Jesus only gave a loud cry and "breathed his last." Mark's account parallels Matthew's (Mark 15:36).

What then shall we make of Jesus in Psalm 69? At least this: Jesus himself was familiar with the psalm, and so were the writers of the New Testament. Just as Psalm 22 clearly seems to unlock the inner struggle of Jesus on the cross, Psalm 69 not only does this but extends it to his entry into Jerusalem.

Nonetheless, when it comes to seeing Jesus in Psalm 69, we are presented with a puzzle. It is not just the confession of guilt in verse 5 that troubles us. How could Jesus internalize those awful curses of verses 22-28? We turn now to that.

JESUS AND CRIES FOR VENGEANCE

Darkened eyes, trembling loins, burning anger, desolated camps, being blotted out of the book of the living: so unsavory are these metaphors and their meaning that one scholar refuses to repeat them in his commentary, referring only to the verses by number. Likewise, C. S. Lewis says, "In some of the Psalms the spirit of hatred which strikes us in the face is like the heat from a furnace mouth." Lewis is reluctant to dwell on these curses, but I think that it may not be such a bad idea. For one thing, Jesus must have done so. For another, they show us that the ancient Israelites were no less human than ourselves. Shocked as we may tell ourselves we are when we read the curses, we know down deep that we too have such thoughts. One of the most tenderhearted people I know, when she hears of human atrocities, wonders why God doesn't just strike the perpetrators dead; *she* would. Knowing that the psalmists themselves could issue such death-dealing words is a comfort. David was a man after God's own heart, the Scriptures say (1 Samuel 13:14; Acts 13:22). Can we be worse than David? Does not God's response to David give us hope?

Our indignation, however, is often triggered by personal affronts to us, our friends, our community, our compatriots. We are not concerned for God but ourselves. As Dietrich Bonhoeffer notes, "The enemies referred to here [in the cursing sections of the psalms] are the enemies of the cause of God, who lay hands on us for the sake of God. It is nowhere a matter of personal conflict." Nor do the psalmists take vengeance into their own hands. They leave it in the hands of God. They can fully display the vindictive emotions they feel because when they leave vengeance with God, they have left it in the hands of the one who judges in both utter righteousness and utter mercy. Everyone from the most ordinary of sinners to the philandering, murdering David, to Peter who denied Christ, to the thief on the cross—everyone who wishes can come under the mercy of God.

Still, we are taken aback when we think of Jesus absorbing this psalm. Remember that he knew this psalm. We know he associated himself with the agony of the psalmist in verse 9. He would also have dealt with the profound cursing verses (vv. 22-28). What was his reaction? We know that he did not respond with vengeance against his enemies. How did he feel when hit by these verbal blasts from the furnace mouth?

I suggest that he was seeing in Psalm 22 and 69 two complementary things. On the one hand, he was seeing just how profoundly troubled, even how desperately evil, we fallen human beings can be. Second, he was seeing beneath it all how fundamental our desire for goodness and righteousness is. In this world where evil is so pervasive, we cannot have one without the other. Our fallenness keeps our justified anger from being fully righteous. But God is not constrained by our character, and neither was Jesus. He was tempted as all of us are—tempted to cry out for sudden vengeance—but he didn't. He was tempted yet remained without sin (Hebrews 4:15).

I think, too, that as he saw the results of the evil in our hearts, he came to realize the role he would have to play in our redemption. He would bear the guilt of our guilty anger and vindictiveness. On the cross he did so. "Jesus Christ himself requests the execution of the wrath of God on his body," says Bonhoeffer, "and thus he leads me back daily to the gravity and grace of his cross for me and all enemies of God." What must have been the incredible pain of that!

Finally, of course, the story of history does not end on the cross or even in the resurrection. There will be an end to this age, a time when the Lord Jesus Christ will come with the sword of justice. Then the vengeance that is God's becomes the righteous vengeance of our Lord. Meanwhile, we live in the in-between time—the already and the not yet. We sinfully cry out for immediate vengeance, but our plea will be answered with utter justice only in God's good time. Meanwhile, as we contemplate the vivid images of verses 21-28 and penetrate into the deep mysteries of Psalm 69, we participate in the anger of the psalmist as he makes his case, inappropriate as it may seem to be.

With this in mind, let us pray the psalm.

PRAYING PSALM 69

Read the entire psalm aloud slowly; then pray it section by section.

> [1]Save me, O God,
>   for the waters have come up to my neck.
> [2]I sink in deep mire,
>   where there is no foothold;
> I have come into deep waters,
>   and the flood sweeps over me.
> [3]I am weary with my crying;
>   my throat is parched.

My eyes grow dim
   with waiting for my God.

Respond: Lord, I read this psalm and hear the voice of David. I know about some of his deep troubles. But mostly I think of the situation that is expressed with such vivid images. I picture a man sunk deep in mud with waves washing over him. Wet as he is, his throat is parched. In such a desperate situation he cries out, like Jesus on the cross, "I thirst." Then I think of Jesus, who really said these words and for whom on the cross the images seem so apt. There is David waiting for God to save him. There is Israel—both ancient and first-century, and by extension even today—waiting for God to come. Eyes growing dim, perception lagging, terror threatening, God absent: this is the condition of almost total despair. *Pause to let this sink in. Then continue.*

There are times when I too have felt this way. *If you do so now, pour out your soul to God with specific details. He knows them, but speaking them out will eventually lead you to leave them with God for his solution.*

And I know others—some friends, some I only know about—who are in despair. May I leave with you their request for comfort? Yes, I do so now. *(Bring their names before God.)*

   [4]More in number than the hairs of my head
      are those who hate me without cause;
   many are those who would destroy me,
      my enemies who accuse me falsely.

Respond: David and Jesus both were hated without cause, falsely accused of all manner of misdeeds. *If this has happened to you and you are still upset, tell God the details. If your friends are in this situation, lay their troubles before the Lord.*

What I did not steal
    must I now restore?
[5]O God, you know my folly;
    the wrongs I have done are not hidden from you.

Respond: Yes, Lord, you know my folly. *Mention some of your foolish actions. Then pause.*

[6]Do not let those who hope in you be put to shame because of me,
    O Lord GOD of hosts;
 do not let those who seek you be dishonored because of me,
    O God of Israel.

Respond: Pray for those who may have suffered because of what you have done or left undone.

[7]It is for your sake that I have borne reproach,
    that shame has covered my face.

Respond: This was surely true for David and for Jesus. *Can you say this for yourself? If so, do so with some of the details.*

[8]I have become a stranger to my kindred,
    an alien to my mother's children.

Respond: Lord, here are those from whom I feel so estranged. *Name names.* Lord, may we be reconciled! *Pause.*

[9]It is zeal for your house that has consumed me;
    the insults of those who insult you have fallen on me.

Respond: For David and Jesus, this was a focal point of the psalm. May I too have a zeal for your kingdom! May I be ready for the embarrassment I may be to my friends! *Bring before the Lord those* matters that have earned you the insults of others. *Pray for strength to maintain your integrity and your devotion to Christ and his kingdom.* One paraphraser of this verse wrote, "I love you more than I can say. . . . I'm madly in love with you." May this be true of me! And may I gladly take the blame "for everything [your enemies] dislike about you."

> [10]When I humbled my soul with fasting,
>> they insulted me for doing so.
> [11]When I made sackcloth my clothing,
>> I became a byword to them.
> [12]I am the subject of gossip for those who sit in the gate,
>> and the drunkards make songs about me.

Respond: Lord Jesus, I see you in Jerusalem, teaching, healing, befriending the down and out, those oppressed by the system. I see those around you throwing out insults and using their wit to compose satirical ditties about you. *Pause.*

> [13]But as for me, my prayer is to you, O LORD.
>> At an acceptable time, O God,
>>> in the abundance of your steadfast love, answer me.
>> With your faithful help [14]rescue me
>>> from sinking in the mire;
>> let me be delivered from my enemies
>>> and from the deep waters.
> [15]Do not let the flood sweep over me,
>> or the deep swallow me up,
>> or the Pit close its mouth over me.

Respond: These words are my prayer! *Pause.*

> [16]Answer me, O LORD, for your steadfast love is good;

according to your abundant mercy, turn to me.
    ¹⁷Do not hide your face from your servant,
        for I am in distress—make haste to answer me.
    ¹⁸Draw near to me, redeem me,
        set me free because of my enemies.

Respond: These words too are not just for David and Jesus. They are
mine.

    ¹⁹You know the insults I receive,
        and my shame and dishonor;
        my foes are all known to you.
    ²⁰Insults have broken my heart,
        so that I am in despair.
    I looked for pity, but there was none;
        and for comforters, but I found none.
    ²¹They gave me poison for food,
        and for my thirst they gave me vinegar to drink.

Respond: Again I see Jesus on the cross. I hear him cry out, "My God,
my God, why have you forsaken me?" I hear him say, "I thirst." *Pause.*

    ²²Let their table be a trap for them,
        a snare for their allies.
    ²³Let their eyes be darkened so that they cannot see,
        and make their loins tremble continually.
    ²⁴Pour out your indignation upon them,
        and let your burning anger overtake them.
    ²⁵May their camp be a desolation;
        let no one live in their tents.
    ²⁶For they persecute those whom you have struck down,
        and those whom you have wounded, they attack still more.

²⁷Add guilt to their guilt;
>   may they have no acquittal from you.
²⁸Let them be blotted out of the book of the living;
>   let them not be enrolled among the righteous.

Respond: Lord, these are awful words to say, awful thoughts to contemplate. Yet in my anguish, this attitude is mine too. Surely those who reject and oppose you deserve the harshest of judgment. But then so do I, for both the little ways I stray from your straight and narrow and the big ways I hurt you by hurting people with my words and my actions. *Mention some of these here.* I can easily imagine them as the words of David, for his fallen humanity is mine. But I cannot imagine Jesus praying these verses. I rejoice, however, that he took into himself all the guilt of David's and my sinful character and misguided moral indignation. May I see beneath and behind these vindictive requests the psalmist's earnest desire for your righteous and merciful judgment to prevail.

²⁹But I am lowly and in pain;
>   let your salvation, O God, protect me.

Respond: This, Lord, is the last time in this prayer that I will be asking you for deliverance, for I know how this prayer goes. I will soon be sounding your praise. I pray in hope, and I see that hope realized.

³⁰I will praise the name of God with a song;
>   I will magnify him with thanksgiving.
³¹This will please the LORD more than an ox
>   or a bull with horns and hoofs.
³²Let the oppressed see it and be glad;
>   you who seek God, let your hearts revive.
³³For the LORD hears the needy,

and does not despise his own that are in bonds.

Respond: This, Lord, is my prayer. *Pause, then slowly reread verses 30-33 as that prayer. Then continue with the closing verses.*

> [34]Let heaven and earth praise him,
>> the seas and everything that moves in them.
> [35]For God will save Zion
>> and rebuild the cities of Judah;
> and his servants shall live there and possess it;
> [36] the children of his servants shall inherit it,
>> and those who love his name shall live in it.

Respond: What a glorious conclusion this is! Let the heavens proclaim the glory of God and the earth echo its praise! The psalmist foresaw the rebuilding of Israel. Jesus proclaimed and embodied the coming kingdom of God. I can envision both of them. Even so, Maranatha! Come, Lord Jesus! Amen.

Small Group Study of Psalm 69

The following comments are directed to the leader.

Introduction

As you will have seen already, this psalm is longer than most we have prayed. Perhaps you should warn the participants that it may take longer than usual to prepare to pray it. Not to worry. Take two sessions, reserving the second session for a review of the psalm and for more than the usual time for prayer.

Group Instruction and Questions

1. Have one person read Psalm 69 at an ordinary pace.

2. Have a second person read the psalm slowly, pausing briefly after each verse.

3. Have another person reread the psalm at an ordinary pace.

4. What verses strike you as you read and reread the psalm? (Give the group time to review the psalm silently and then take their answers. These are likely to involve verses with vivid imagery evoking sympathy with the psalmist [verses 1-5 and 19-21] and those given over to cursing. Keep the conversation from dealing with the cursing at this point. That will come later.)

5. What is the general flow of the ideas? (Participants who have studied the earlier psalms should be able to figure this out for themselves. If help is needed, see pp. 114-15.)

6. How does the psalmist feel about his predicament? Where does his anger break out? In what frame of mind does the psalm end? Why?

7. What do you think explains the violent imagery of verses 22-28?

Is the anger understandable? Is the anger justified? Explain.

8. When Jesus prayed this psalm, how do you think he dealt with the cursing? (This is a crucial question to consider. You may wish to use some of the explanation of this given on pp. 120-22.)

9. Why is verse 9 regarding "zeal for your house" so important within the framework of this psalm? Why did the early church find the verse significant? (See John 2:13-22.)

10. Why might we wish to take verse 9 as a core orientation for our own life? Listen to Eugene Peterson's translation: "I love you more than I can say. / Because I'm madly in love with you, / They blame me for everything they dislike about you." How does that help us with the question of core orientation?

11. What other verses in this psalm do we find reflected in the Gospels? (Verse 4, they "hate me without cause" [John 15:25]; verse 21, "vinegar to drink" [Matthew 27:34, 48; Mark 15:36; John 19:28-29].)

12. In what ways is Psalm 69 like Psalm 22? Consider first the structure of these two psalms and, second, two specific verses (verses 4 and 21). (For help here, see pp. 120-22.)

13. In what ways is Psalm 69 applicable to us today? Why do you think it is appropriate for us to pray it?

When the group is ready to pray the psalm, you may find the following liturgy helpful. Still, if your normal time for this study is consumed, why not take an extra session to review and then pray the psalm? The goal of prayer is not to get everything prayed at one time but to return again and again to pray and repray from a growing sense of who God is, what he wants for us and what he wants from us.

Directed Prayer

The following script may help the group to pray the psalm.

Leader: Let us pray Psalm 69 together.

>¹Save me, O God,
>>for the waters have come up to my neck.
>
>²I sink in deep mire,
>>where there is no foothold;
>
> I have come into deep waters,
>>and the flood sweeps over me.
>
>³I am weary with my crying;
>>my throat is parched.
>
> My eyes grow dim
>>with waiting for my God.

Leader: Lord, we read this psalm and hear the voice of David. We know about some of his deep troubles. But mostly we do not think of David in particular but the situation expressed in such vivid images. Picture a man sunk deep in mud with waves washing over him. Wet as he is, his throat is parched. (*Pause.*) In such a desperate situation the man cries out, "I thirst." Then think of Jesus, who really said these words and for whom the images seem so apt. (*Pause.*) Think then of David waiting for God to save him. (*Pause.*) Think of Israel—both ancient and first-century, and by extension even today—waiting for God to come. Eyes growing dim, perception lagging, terror threatening, God absent: this is the condition of almost total despair. (*Pause to let this sink in. Then continue.*)

There are times when we too have felt this way. If you feel it now, pour out your soul to God with specific details. He knows them, but your bringing them to mind will eventually help you to leave them with God for his solution. (*Pause.*)

And there are others—some friends, some we only know about—who are in despair. We leave with you their request for comfort. In silence present them before God. (*Pause.*)

> [4]More in number than the hairs of my head
>> are those who hate me without cause;
> many are those who would destroy me,
>> my enemies who accuse me falsely.

Leader: David and Jesus both were hated without cause, falsely accused of all manner of misdeeds. If this has happened to you and you are still upset, tell God the details. If your friends are in this situation, lay their troubles before the Lord. (*Pause.*)

> What I did not steal
>> must I now restore?
> [5]O God, you know my folly;
>> the wrongs I have done are not hidden from you.

Leader: Yes, Lord, you know our folly. Think of some of your own. (*Pause.*)

> [6]Do not let those who hope in you be put to shame because of me,
>> O Lord GOD of hosts;
> do not let those who seek you be dishonored because of me,
>> O God of Israel.

Leader: Pray silently for those who may have suffered because of what you have done or left undone.

> [7]It is for your sake that I have borne reproach,
>> that shame has covered my face.

Leader: This was surely true for David and for Jesus too. Can you say this for yourself? If so, do so silently with some of the details. *(Pause.)*

> ⁸I have become a stranger to my kindred,
>> an alien to my mother's children.

Leader: Lord, here are those from whom I feel so estranged. Name names silently. *(Pause.)* Lord, may we be reconciled!

> ⁹It is zeal for your house that has consumed me;
>> the insults of those who insult you have fallen on me.

Leader: For David and Jesus, this was a focal point of the psalm. May we too have zeal for your kingdom! May we be ready for the embarrassment this may be before our friends! Bring before the Lord those matters that have earned you the insults of others. Pray for strength to maintain your integrity and your devotion to Christ and his kingdom. *(Pause.)* As Eugene Peterson translates this verse, "I love you more than I can say. . . . I'm madly in love with you." May this be true of us! And may we gladly take the blame "for everything [your enemies] dislike about you."

> ¹⁰When I humbled my soul with fasting,
>> they insulted me for doing so.
> ¹¹When I made sackcloth my clothing,
>> I became a byword to them.
> ¹²I am the subject of gossip for those who sit in the gate,
>> and the drunkards make songs about me.

Leader: Picture Jesus in your mind's eye. There he is in Jerusalem, teaching, healing, befriending the down and out, those oppressed by the system. See those around him throwing out insults and using their wit to compose satirical ditties about him. *(Pause.)*

   [13]But as for me, my prayer is to you, O LORD.
       At an acceptable time, O God,
       in the abundance of your steadfast love, answer me.
     With your faithful help [14]rescue me
       from sinking in the mire;
     let me be delivered from my enemies
       and from the deep waters.
   [15]Do not let the flood sweep over me,
       or the deep swallow me up,
       or the Pit close its mouth over me.

Leader: These words are our prayer! *(Pause.)*

   [16]Answer me, O LORD, for your steadfast love is good;
       according to your abundant mercy, turn to me.
   [17]Do not hide your face from your servant,
       for I am in distress—make haste to answer me.
   [18]Draw near to me, redeem me,
       set me free because of my enemies.

Leader: These words too are not just for David and Jesus. They are
also ours.

   [19]You know the insults I receive,
       and my shame and dishonor;
       my foes are all known to you.
   [20]Insults have broken my heart,
       so that I am in despair.
     I looked for pity, but there was none;
       and for comforters, but I found none.
   [21]They gave me poison for food,
       and for my thirst they gave me vinegar to drink.

Leader: Again, see Jesus on the cross. Hear him cry out, "My God, my God, why have you forsaken me?" Hear him say, "I thirst." Hear him say, "For my thirst they gave me vinegar." *(Pause.)*

²²Let their table be a trap for them,
     a snare for their allies.
²³Let their eyes be darkened so that they cannot see,
     and make their loins tremble continually.
²⁴Pour out your indignation upon them,
     and let your burning anger overtake them.
²⁵May their camp be a desolation;
     let no one live in their tents.
²⁶For they persecute those whom you have struck down,
     and those whom you have wounded, they attack still more.
²⁷Add guilt to their guilt;
     may they have no acquittal from you.
²⁸Let them be blotted out of the book of the living;
     let them not be enrolled among the righteous.

Leader: Lord, these are awful words to say, awful thoughts to contemplate. Yet sometimes we too think these thoughts. Surely those who reject and oppose you deserve the harshest of judgment. But then so does each of us—for both the little ways we stray from your straight and narrow and the big ways we hurt you by hurting others with our words and our actions. Mention some of these in silence. *(Pause.)* We can easily imagine these curses in the mouth of David, for his fallen humanity is ours too. But we cannot imagine Jesus praying these verses. We can, however, rejoice that he took into himself all the guilt of David's and our sinful character and misguided moral indignation. May we see beneath and behind these vindictive requests the psalmist's earnest desire for your righteous and merciful judgment to prevail.

²⁹But I am lowly and in pain;

> let your salvation, O God, protect me.

Leader: This, Lord, is the last time we will be asking you for deliverance, for we know how this psalm ends. We will soon be sounding your praise. We sound it now.

³⁰I will praise the name of God with a song;

> I will magnify him with thanksgiving.

³¹This will please the LORD more than an ox

> or a bull with horns and hoofs.

³²Let the oppressed see it and be glad;

> you who seek God, let your hearts revive.

³³For the LORD hears the needy,

> and does not despise his own that are in bonds.

Leader: This, Lord, is our prayer. *(Pause, then slowly reread verses 30-33 as that prayer. Then continue with the closing verses.)*

³⁴Let heaven and earth praise him,

> the seas and everything that moves in them.

³⁵For God will save Zion

> and rebuild the cities of Judah;

> and his servants shall live there and possess it;

³⁶   the children of his servants shall inherit it,

> and those who love his name shall live in it.

Leader: What a glorious conclusion this is! Let the heavens proclaim the glory of God and the earth echo its praise! The psalmist foresaw the rebuilding of Israel. Jesus foresaw and embodied the coming kingdom of God. We can envision both of them. Even so, Maranatha! Come, Lord Jesus! Amen.

PART TWO

The Psalms in Jesus

6

HE RIDES UPON THE STORM

Psalm 29

Up from the western horizon loomed three thunderheads—not an unusual occurrence on the open plains of northern Nebraska, but one that sent chills up my spine. I was a young boy then, living on a ranch and assigned the duty of bringing in the cows for milking. As these three cloud columns came closer and closer and rose higher and higher, I wondered if I was being pursued by the Father, the Son and the Holy Ghost.

David the psalmist must have had something of the same experience as the young shepherd boy who would someday be both king and poet laureate of Israel. In any case, prompted by the Holy Spirit from somewhere in David's imagination sprang the text of this marvelous psalm. Though the psalm is not considered messianic and is nowhere quoted in the New Testament, can it too be a psalm of Jesus? Let us see.

PSALM 29

The Voice of God in a Great Storm
A Psalm of David.

> [1]Ascribe to the LORD, O heavenly beings,

ascribe to the LORD glory and strength.
^{2}Ascribe to the LORD the glory of his name;
worship the LORD in holy splendor.

^{3}The voice of the LORD is over the waters;
the God of glory thunders,
the LORD, over mighty waters.
^{4}The voice of the LORD is powerful;
the voice of the LORD is full of majesty.

^{5}The voice of the LORD breaks the cedars;
the LORD breaks the cedars of Lebanon.
^{6}He makes Lebanon skip like a calf,
and Sirion like a young wild ox.

^{7}The voice of the LORD flashes forth flames of fire.
^{8}The voice of the LORD shakes the wilderness;
the LORD shakes the wilderness of Kadesh.

^{9}The voice of the LORD causes the oaks to whirl,
and strips the forest bare;
and in his temple all say, "Glory!"

^{10}The LORD sits enthroned over the flood;
the LORD sits enthroned as king forever.
^{11}May the LORD give strength to his people!
May the LORD bless his people with peace!

GETTING AT THE MEANING OF PSALM 29

What a dramatic psalm this is! Booming thunder, flashing lightning, hurricane winds, earth quaking, forest trees stripped bare and snapped off—and behind and above it all God is seated on his throne and riding above the storm, in control of all heaven and earth. No wonder everyone in God's temple shouts, "Glory!"

But before we get too carried away by the excitement of the moment, let us see how the psalm is structured and thus see just why it works to produce those emotions we experience in our reading.

After struggling with the complex structure of Psalm 69, it is a relief to come to a psalm that is both simple and clear in basic meaning and structure. Still, there are dimensions that may not be obvious from our initial readings.

Rational Structure

Call to the angels to ascribe glory to the Lord, verses 1-2

Power of God's voice (over the seas), verses 3-4

Power of God's voice (over the earth), verses 5-9

The Lord as king (over heaven and earth), verse 10

Prayer (for strength and peace from the God of glory), verse 11

First notice how the psalm has both a panoramic cosmic sweep and a geographic sweep. On the one hand it begins in the heavens, descends to the earth, then reascends to heaven, from which strength and peace are to come back to earth. On the other hand it pictures a storm that begins over the Mediterranean on the west and sweeps east toward the plains and mountains of Israel. Then, starting in Lebanon and Sirion (Mt. Hermon) in the north, it sweeps across Israel to the southern wilderness of Kadesh. The whole of Israel is encompassed in the glory of the Lord.

Second, notice how the psalm begins with the personal (the Lord and the heavenly beings), moves to the impersonal (the sea, the forests, the land) and returns to the personal (the Lord and his people).

Third, the psalm moves from the glory of God as such to the manifestations of this glory seen in God's power over nature, then on to the effect of this glory and power to give "strength" (fits with God's power) and "peace" (fits with God's character—what he finally does with his power). This movement may be most significant as we pray the psalm for ourselves.

The psalm is indeed a little poetic gem, a gem that is best seen as a hymn, one used in the worship of the ancient Israelites and imitated to some extent by such classic Christian hymns as this one by William Cowper (1731-1800):

> God moves in a mysterious way,
>   His wonders to perform;
> He plants His footsteps in the sea,
>   And rides upon the storm.

The psalm has also prompted purple prose from preachers like Robert Murray M'Cheyne and Charles Spurgeon. It's difficult to speak about it without launching into an alliterating litany of literary lines. But I digress, sort of.

The Voice of David and Israel

As we revel in the gleams shot from this bright jewel, we ought not forget that first of all, this is a psalm of David and Israel. Without help from scholars, we would probably not be aware that in the background of this psalm lies the Canaanite cultures that surrounded and often penetrated that of the Hebrews.

Baal, the weather god of the Canaanites, was believed to have brought chaos under control. "He is portrayed in Ugaritic iconography with lightning as a weapon in his hand." But Psalm 29 asserts that all the forces of nature that the Canaanites attributed to Baal are really under the control of Yahweh. Similarly, Yam, "the deified *flood* or *sea* of Canaanite tradition has become merely the inanimate tool of the Lord." In other words, Psalm 29 demythologizes the pagan gods; they are not in control of an earth self-endowed with gods and goddesses. Rather the earth, including all its powers, is an impersonal tool in the control of Yahweh.

At the same time that we distinguish between Yahweh and the Canaanite gods, we must distinguish between Yahweh and what many in our culture call nature, the physical reality that science can explain without reference to any God at all. John Calvin saw this long ago. Philosophers have so separated God from his creation that they treat it as autonomous, capable of being known without regard to its Creator. Would that scientists like Richard Dawkins of *The Blind Watchmaker* fame take this comment to heart!

Psalm 29 forces us all to choose. Whom will we serve with our whole body, mind and spirit? For the ancients it was either the immanent and deified personal forces of nature or the God of Abraham, Isaac and Jacob. For us the choices are one of the many popular immanent gods of the East or the New Age, the secular god of impersonal nature, or again, the God of Abraham, Isaac and Jacob. In praying this psalm we choose the God of Abraham, Isaac and Jacob.

The Voice of Jesus

How then would Jesus pray this psalm? Would he too not see the contrast drawn by the psalmist? Would he too not take the opportunity afforded by this psalm to lift his mind and heart into the glory of the Father? Would he not receive the sense of growing certitude that he was integrally associated with this victorious God who held everything in his control?

Think of Jesus in the wilderness (Luke 4:1-13). Storms came up in the wilderness of Kadesh. Storms come up almost everywhere on earth. How did he react to them? And how did Jesus react to Satan, who for forty days tempted him as he grew weaker and weaker from hunger? Besieged by the great accuser, the great deceiver, would he not remember and be strengthened by the testimony of Psalm 29? God is in control of all circumstances. He is to be trusted regardless of the danger. Would Jesus not ascribe glory to the Father who plants his footsteps in the sea and rides upon the storm? We cannot know, of course, but we can imagine the answer.

Think, too, of Jesus asleep in the boat on the Sea of Galilee (Mark 4:35-41). A violent storm comes up. He is awakened by his disciples and calmly calms the sea. "Peace! Be still!" he says. "Why are you afraid? Have you still no faith?" He seems already to have seen how much he and his Father are one.

When Jesus meditated on the call of Psalm 29 to ascribe glory to God, did he substitute himself for Yahweh? He did that sort of thing elsewhere in the Gospels, so perhaps he did so with this psalm too. Certainly we can see him in the psalm. In a real sense Jesus, the Word of God made flesh, is "the voice of the LORD" in Psalm 29—this phrase appears seven times and is the focus of God's character in this particular psalm.

Psalm 29 as Our Voice

So we come to Psalm 29 as our answering speech. How do we pray the psalm? For one thing, we can do what the heavenly host is called to do—give glory to God. But what does it mean to give glory? How can we do that?

In the Bible, *glory* is the expression of God's character, his holiness—in other words, his separateness from all creation, not just from the sticks and stones but from the flora, the fauna and especially us. If God appears to us, we do not so much "see" him as "see" the glory emanating from him. So, then, how can we give God what he already has? Perhaps we could say that we give God glory as we worship in church or acknowledge his awesome and holy character in verbal prayer and ritual action. But I think there is more to giving God glory than to do so in specifically religious forms. I have found Karl Barth's comments about God's glory especially helpful: "God does not need to make any fuss about his glory: God is glorious. He simply needs to show Himself as He is. He simply needs to reveal himself. That is what He does in man."

So how do we glorify God? The idea is simple. When we live as we should, we display in our life the character of God. To glorify God, then, should be a deliberate act, something we must intentionally learn to do and then do.

To put it in more concrete terms, we know God primarily by knowing and understanding Jesus. Then we display in our life the character of God displayed in the life of Jesus. The idea is simple, isn't it? But the execution is profoundly difficult. Only by God's grace is it possible at all.

But that is what we should do—ascribe glory to God by living like Jesus. It is not so much "what would Jesus do?" Rather, what would Jesus have us do that reveals his character in our words and attitudes and actions? The way toward an answer to that question will take us to the New Testament, to the Gospels for the example set by Jesus, and to the Letters to see how some of the details have been delineated by the apostles.

Prayer, of course, is always appropriate. So we turn to that.

PRAYING PSALM 29

Read the psalm in its entirety one more time. Then pray.

> [1]Ascribe to the LORD, O heavenly beings,
>   ascribe to the LORD glory and strength.
> [2]Ascribe to the LORD the glory of his name;
>   worship the LORD in holy splendor.

Respond: You are glory and strength and honor and are encompassed in holy splendor. How can either the angels or I give you anything you don't already have? But you ask us to do so, and so I do so now. *In your own words express your delight in God, and pause in silence as you let your mind rest in God's glory. Then pray:* Lord, I know that the best way for me to give you glory is to live so that more and more I come to express the character of Jesus. Paul said to the church in Corinth that they had the mind of Christ. May that word become true in me!

> [3]The voice of the LORD is over the waters;
>   the God of glory thunders,
>   the LORD, over mighty waters.
> [4]The voice of the LORD is powerful;
>   the voice of the LORD is full of majesty.

Respond: Picture this scene in your mind—the storm, the thunder. Hear the voice of the Lord thunder behind and above the storm. Pause.

> [5]The voice of the LORD breaks the cedars;
>   the LORD breaks the cedars of Lebanon.

Respond: See the forests—giant cedar trees on the foothills of the mountains of northern Israel. See them being stripped and falling like toothpicks. *Recall any experience you have had in and around a hurricane or violent storm. Do you hear the voice of the Lord? Remember, he is in control. He is there! Pause to hear the voice.*

> ⁶He makes Lebanon skip like a calf,
>   and Sirion like a young wild ox.

Respond: Now feel the earth shake under you. See the hills stripped bare, dancing like a herd of cattle as the ground swells and falls away under them. Do you feel it swell and fall away under you too? Pause to let it do so.

> ⁷The voice of the LORD flashes forth flames of fire.
> ⁸The voice of the LORD shakes the wilderness;
>   the LORD shakes the wilderness of Kadesh.

Respond: Now, Lord, I see lightning flash and hear thunder crash. I see the wilderness of Israel shaking like a leaf.

> ⁹The voice of the LORD causes the oaks to whirl,
>   and strips the forest bare;
>   and in his temple all say, "Glory!"

Respond: I see the storm now reaching its climax. In Jerusalem I hear the people with one stupendous voice, though a paltry imitation of yours, cry out "Glory!" I see the church down through the ages sing as the angels sang, "Glory to God in the highest!"

> ¹⁰The LORD sits enthroned over the flood;
>   the LORD sits enthroned as king forever.

Respond: High and lifted up, there you are seated on your throne! I know as glorious as it is, it is but a dim shadow of your transcendent presence. O King, forever may I give you glory in the temple of your creation—the earth and its fullness. *Pause.*

And now, here in the temple of your creation, I say, "Glory to God in the highest!" and add, "And on earth peace among those whom he favors."

[11]May the LORD give strength to his people!
    May the LORD bless his people with peace!

Respond: Amen.

Small Group Study of Psalm 29

The following comments are directed to the leader.

Group Questions

1. Have one person read Psalm 29 in its entirety at an ordinary pace.

2. Have another person read it very slowly, with a pause after each verse.

3. A third reading would be appropriate but not if it looks as if people in the group are getting restless.

4. What strikes you most about the psalm? The ideas? The images? The emotions?

5. Have any of you experienced a storm like the one described here? What was your greatest concern at the time? How has this experience affected your life? Were you able to see God in your storm? *(This question may prompt a lot of discussion as participants relive some rather fearful times. The point of the question is to get people to see that events have different meanings for different people, but the common thread is that God is in control even when we don't see him in action.)*

6. Have someone describe the structure of the psalm. (For help, see p. 141.)

7. In what tone is the psalm written? In what verse does the climax come? How does this help us to discern the main theme of the psalm? What is that theme?

8. Under what circumstances would this psalm be a fitting one to pray? Why?

9. Why is the final verse a fitting close to the psalm? What reasons does the psalm give us for thinking the Lord will answer the prayer of verse 11?

When you feel that the group is ready for corporate prayer, you may use this liturgy.

Directed Prayer

The following script may help the group to pray the psalm.

Leader: Let us pray Psalm 29 together.

> ¹Ascribe to the LORD, O heavenly beings,
>> ascribe to the LORD glory and strength.
> ²Ascribe to the LORD the glory of his name;
>> worship the LORD in holy splendor.

Leader: Lord, you are glory and strength and honor. You are surrounded by holy splendor. How can either the angels or we give you anything you don't already have? But you ask us to do so, and so we give you glory now. Silently and in your own words express your delight in God. *(Pause, then pray:)* Lord, I know that the best way for us to give you glory is to live so that more and more we come to express the image of Jesus. Paul said to the believers in Corinth that they had the mind of Christ. May that word become true in this small community! *(Brief pause.)*

> ³The voice of the LORD is over the waters;
>> the God of glory thunders,
>> the LORD, over mighty waters.
> ⁴The voice of the LORD is powerful;
>> the voice of the LORD is full of majesty.

Leader: Picture this scene in your mind—the storm, the thunder. Hear the voice of the Lord thunder behind and above the storm. *(Pause.)*

> ⁵The voice of the LORD breaks the cedars;

the LORD breaks the cedars of Lebanon.

Leader: See the forests—giant cedar trees on the foothills of the mountains of northern Israel. See them being stripped and falling like toothpicks. Recall any experience you have had in and around a hurricane or violent storm. Do you hear the voice of the Lord? Remember, he is in control. He was there! He is here. Let us keep silence as we pause to hear his voice. *(Pause.)*

> [6]He makes Lebanon skip like a calf,
>   and Sirion like a young wild ox.
> [7]The voice of the LORD flashes forth flames of fire.
> [8]The voice of the LORD shakes the wilderness;
>   the LORD shakes the wilderness of Kadesh.

Leader: Now feel the earth shake under you. See the hills now stripped bare, dancing like a herd of cattle as the ground swells and falls away under them. Do you feel it swell and fall away under you too? *(Pause to let it do so.)* Now see the lightning flash and hear thunder crash. See the wilderness of Israel shaking like a leaf. *(Pause.)*

> [9]The voice of the LORD causes the oaks to whirl,
>   and strips the forest bare;
>   and in his temple all say, "Glory!"

Leader: See the storm now reaching its climax. Hear the people in the temple in Jerusalem cry with one stupendous voice, "Glory!" See Jesus at prayer in the wilderness cry out, "Glory!" See the church down through the ages sing as the angels sang, "Glory to God in the highest!" *(Brief pause.)*

> [10]The LORD sits enthroned over the flood;
>   the LORD sits enthroned as king forever.

Leader: We see you, Lord, high and lifted up. You are there seated on your throne! We know that as glorious as this vision is, it is but a dim shadow of your transcendent presence. O King, forever may we give you glory in the place we are now. And may we give glory at all times in the temple of your creation—the earth and its fullness. *(Pause.)*

Now here in this place we say, "Glory to God in the highest." And we add, "On earth peace among those whom he favors." *(Then say together the final verse.)*

[11]May the LORD give strength to his people!
    May the LORD bless his people with peace!

Leader: Amen.

7

The Lord Is My Shepherd

Psalm 23

"The Lord is my shepherd." These words must resonate with every Christian, so familiar they are. And what do we imagine when we hear them? Surely, at least for my generation, it is paintings and drawings of Jesus holding a lamb and surrounded by well-scrubbed children. We saw them in Sunday school and cannot forget them. Romantic, idealistic, almost ethereal, these images arise unbidden when as adults we hear or read the psalm again.

Jesus is, of course, the Good Shepherd. This psalm does summon up feelings of comfort that would suggest such images even if they were not first prompted by nineteenth-century art. But if we are to be serious about how to pray this psalm, we shall have to look afresh at what it really meant to be a shepherd in ancient Israel. Moreover, refreshing our experience of the psalm will do us much good. So let us read it again several times.

PSALM 23

The Divine Shepherd

A Psalm of David.

> [1]The LORD is my shepherd, I shall not want.
> [2] He makes me lie down in green pastures;
>   he leads me beside still waters;
> [3] he restores my soul.
>   He leads me in right paths
>   for his name's sake.
>
> [4]Even though I walk through the darkest valley,
>   I fear no evil;
> for you are with me;
>   your rod and your staff—
>   they comfort me.
>
> [5]You prepare a table before me
>   in the presence of my enemies;
> you anoint my head with oil;
>   my cup overflows.
> [6]Surely goodness and mercy shall follow me
>   all the days of my life,
> and I shall dwell in the house of the LORD
>   my whole life long.

GETTING AT THE MEANING OF PSALM 23

When we have entered into the spirit of the psalm, we are ready to enter into its mind, the way it is structured and the details that contribute to the marvelous effect it has had on millions of readers from ancient Israel to the twenty-first century.

Rational Structure

The Lord as shepherd (direct declaration of the central idea), verse 1

What the shepherd does now (immediate effect), verses 2-3

What the shepherd will do (future effect), verse 4

The Lord as host (the image shifts), verse 5

The shepherd and host (long-range effects), verse 6

The psalm opens with a thesis statement that, though stated in the negative, encompasses the entire content of the psalm. There is no need that the Lord does not supply: the Lord supplies everything. Then the psalm fills in the details: what the Lord does now, his effects in the near future, more of his effects now and finally what he does in the long run. In short, he satisfies all our needs.

One of the chief delights of the psalm is its completeness. No further word of comfort is needed. Its application to human life is universal; there is no time or place in which its solace is inappropriate. Whether we are in sickness or in health, alone or in community, young and vibrant or old and gray, at work or at home, the Lord is our shepherd, and he is also our host.

Metaphorical Structure

Many readers familiar with the psalm probably fail to notice the shift in image from the Lord as *shepherd* to the Lord as *host*. The language has sunk deep into our psyches, and an obvious meaning—even if inaccurate—is almost directly perceived. But the shift has puzzled some scholars. Some have wondered if the host should be considered the same as the shepherd, so that verses 5-6 depict in metaphor the feeding of the sheep. But this sort of interpretation complicates the uncomplicated. Why not go with the long tradition of those who simply see the image changing? The Lord is both shepherd and host, not a shepherd who is a host. In the long run, this controversy seems a bit silly. The psalm works magic; let's not toy with how it does so.

SHEPHERDS AND SHEEP

We modern urbanites—most of us around the world are these— know very little about sheep. I imagine that some of us actually get what we know about sheep from Psalm 23 itself and the sentimental Sunday school images of Jesus holding a spotless lamb or reaching with his staff to recover a sheep that has fallen into a mountain crevice. A good antidote is Phillip Keller's *A Shepherd Looks at Psalm 23*. As he proceeds line by line through the psalm, he not only elucidates the work of sheepherding but also sees the immediate applications to our understanding of Jesus, the Good Shepherd, and his relationship to us, his sheep.

Sheep, it turns out, are rather dumb animals. Without a shepherd to direct and restrain them, they stray and get into all sorts of trouble. They are easy prey for wild animals; they are blown about by storms; they lose their way among hills and ravines; they need to be taken to their pastures and returned; they are fragile animals and get deadly diseases. Moreover, to anyone but a shepherd, they stink.

And shepherds themselves are not great noble folk. They know what must be done to tend their flock, but they pick up dirt and grime from the sheep, and they too stink. In the ancient world, they were among the lowest of the low, respected for their work but rejected by polite society. They hardly resembled the images of them we saw when we were young. And at Christmas our children in bathrobes for the church pageant are further barriers to our understanding. It is better to picture shepherds as rough-hewn men carrying a bludgeon for fending off and killing wolves and a long staff with a crook at the end for snagging sheep on the fly or pulling them out of pits. The good shepherd must indeed be a tough character.

At the same time, the sheep really are like us, and the good shepherd really is like Jesus. Made in the image of God and bright as we are, because we have rebelled against God, we are very dumb animals, easily led astray by the machinations of our own inordinate desires. We desperately need to be rescued. And since we not only have sinned but are utter sinners, in the nostrils of God we too stink. Without God as our shepherd, we are lost without hope of recovery. But we are not without hope.

"The Lord is my shepherd, I shall not want." This is the good news. And the details follow:

We look for food on the dry hills (we turn to all the wrong sources seeking a guide to life) . . . he makes us lie down in green pastures.

We befoul our own drinking water (we take what's good, twist it and distort our own lives) . . . he leads us beside still waters.

We lose our souls in sin and foolishness . . . he restores our souls.

We stray among the rocks (we head in all the wrong directions, support all the wrong causes) . . . he leads us on the right paths.

We live for ourselves . . . he empowers us to live for his name's sake.

We live in a dangerous world . . . he guards us with his rod and staff.

But note this: he does not take us out of the dangerous world. Instead he wines and dines us in the very presence of the world that we let squeeze us into its mold.

Indeed, the Lord is our shepherd. His goodness and mercy come to us throughout our lives, and we will dwell in his presence forever.

JESUS AND PSALM 23

Even though the New Testament never directly quotes from Psalm 23, Christians down through the ages have had no difficulty linking Jesus with this psalm. "I am the good shepherd," said Jesus. "The good shepherd lays down his life for the sheep. . . . I know my own and my own know me, just as the Father knows me and I know the Father" (John 10:11, 14-15; see also Hebrews 13:20; 1 Peter 5:4; Revelation 7:17). In saying this, Jesus alluded to the notion in the Hebrew Scriptures that God was the shepherd of Israel (Psalm 77:20; 79:13; 80:1; Ezekiel 34:1-31).

Table fellowship of the host is also important. In societies around the world and even in ours today, inviting someone to dine with you is a sign that you accept them as friends or potential friends, at least as worthy human beings. Did not Jesus have table fellowship with all sorts of lowlife (Mark 2:17)? So low in society did his openness extend that he was accused of being "a glutton and a drunkard, a friend of tax collectors and sinners" (Luke 7:34). Indeed, it could be said that he prepared a table for these outcasts in the presence of their enemies, the religious guardians of propriety. Their enemies became his enemies as well.

Jesus prepared a table for his disciples just before his enemies arrested him. And there was Judas his traitor in their midst. Before the meal was over, however, Judas was excused to do what he had arranged. The "enemy" had been denied the full experience of the Passover feast. But what a feast Jesus gave the remaining faithful disciples in the upper room discourse (John 13:1—17:26)!

In every way Jesus fulfilled this psalm. He embodied in himself all the characteristics of the shepherd of Psalm 23. Though he did not quote from the psalm, he acted it out and thus fulfilled it as much as he did Psalm 22, from which he deliberately quoted.

There is another dimension as well. When Jesus contemplated this psalm, did he think of God the Father as his shepherd? Surely Jesus' attitude toward the Father would fit well with this.

Given these musings, we should now be able to pray Psalm 23 with a greater grasp of its depth.

PRAYING PSALM 23

Read the psalm one more time and then pray.

¹The LORD is my shepherd, I shall not want.

Respond: Lord, you are my shepherd. Dare I say that? Dare I presume upon you, Lord Jesus Christ? What freedom you give me! You want me to be a sheep in your pasture, one of your many, many sheep around the world—both living on earth and in heaven. Thank you for this incredible privilege! Thank you for being the shepherd who has laid down his life for me, and for all of us!

I shall not want for anything that is best for me. I do not presume that you will satisfy all my desires; I may suffer loss of goods, loss of family, loss of the good functioning of heart and lungs, legs and arms. But I know I will not want for anything I ought to want. For what I ought to want is to be one of your flock, listening to your voice, obeying your prompting, glorifying you by showing your character in my life. Lord, you are my shepherd! I shall not want!

² He makes me lie down in green pastures;

Respond: Imagine the scene pictured in verses 2-4. Think of yourself as one of the shepherd's sheep. What do you want? What do you need? Then pray: You, Lord Jesus, Word of God, feed me on your written Word. Green pastures indeed, full of nourishment for body, mind and spirit!

Mention some Scripture that has helped you recently.

he leads me beside still waters;

Respond: In this dry and decadent wasteland of popular culture, you slake my thirst for living water. Amidst the world of simulacra, of ubiquitous TV and endless advertising of things that have no good use either practical or aesthetic, your presence satisfies my longing for genuine reality.

³   he restores my soul.

Respond: You restore my soul. You fill me with the delight of knowing you, of being puzzled by you and your ways, of seeing that I have yet to see so many things about you. I come to you as a broken, distorted image of God. Lord, you are repairing the damage and fitting me for life in your kingdom. Thank you, Lord! Thank you, Jesus! Oh that this restoration would proceed! There is so much more for you to do. *Mention some areas in your life that you know you need help in.* May I be that worthy sheep that bends to your leading!

He leads me in right paths
        for his name's sake.

Respond: You refocus my life, you refine my goals, you head me in the right direction. And you do this not just for me but for the glory it brings to you, to the Father and to the Holy Spirit. *As you remind yourself, tell the Lord some of the specific ways he has directed you—in relationships, in job selection, in tough decisions.*

⁴Even though I walk through the darkest valley,
        I fear no evil;
    for you are with me;

your rod and your staff—
they comfort me.

Respond: Picture yourself as a sheep walking in a dark shadow, the shadow of the valley of death. See the dangers that lurk behind the rocks, the sheep stealers who want you for their flock and will kill to get you. Pause; then pray: You do not take me out of the world. I am now and will be till the end immersed in the cares of the world. Money, sex and power continue to trouble me. But when I turn my attention to you, I realize that the evils of this world are nothing beside your power to save and comfort me. Like every one of your sheep, I have walked through some dark valleys. *Name some of them and be specific.* But you have been with me all along. Help me to realize that at the most profound level of my soul.

[5]You prepare a table before me
in the presence of my enemies;
you anoint my head with oil;
my cup overflows.

Respond: Picture a rich feast, the host having provided beyond your expectation. Pause; then pray: Lord, you give me such joy, even in the fallen world, even when the forces I cannot control put pressure on me to disobey you and live by standards I know are wrong. You sustain me with your presence so that I can ignore those who would wish me ill. *Mention some relevant examples from your life recently.* My cup overflows.

[6]Surely goodness and mercy shall follow me
all the days of my life,
and I shall dwell in the house of the LORD
my whole life long.

Respond: See your life spread out before you, now full of confidence and hope. Pause; then pray: Indeed, Lord, this is the substance of my hope. You are my shepherd. I hear your voice, and I know that you will be with me all of my days—and then throughout eternity. Amen.

Small Group Study of Psalm 23

The following comments are directed to the leader.

Group Questions

1. Have one person read Psalm 23 in its entirety at an ordinary pace.

2. Have another person read it very slowly, with a pause after each verse.

3. A third reading would be appropriate unless it looks as if people in the group are getting restless.

4. Since Psalm 23 is likely to be well known by participants, ask: What has been your experience with Psalm 23? What is your first memory of it? What strikes you most about the psalm? (People may tell a variety of stories. After a few minutes, move on to the next question.)

5. If the psalm has brought comfort, how has it done so?

6. What is the flow of ideas in the psalm? (See p. 155 for help, if needed.)

7. How is the Lord a shepherd? What are sheep like? (See pp. 156-57 for help.) In verses 2-4, what does he do for the sheep? If the Lord is your shepherd, what does he do for you? (This will require participants to interpret the images—feeding, watering, etc.; for help, see p. 157.)

8. How does the image of the Lord change in verse 5? What does the host do? What does the Lord do for you? Do you see him doing this in the presence of your "enemies"?

9. What is the long-run hope that this psalm gives? What does it mean to dwell in the house of the Lord?

When you feel that the group is ready for corporate prayer, you may use the following liturgy.

DIRECTED PRAYER

The following script may help the group to pray the psalm.

Leader: Let us pray Psalm 23 together. *(Read the psalm one more time and then pray.)*

[1]The LORD is my shepherd, I shall not want.

Leader: Lord, you are our shepherd. Dare we say that? Dare we presume upon you, Lord Jesus Christ? What freedom you give us! You want each of us to be a sheep in your pasture, one of your many, many sheep around the world—living on earth or in heaven. Thank you for this incredible privilege! Thank you for being the shepherd who has laid down his life for us!

We shall not want for anything that is best for us. We do not presume that you will satisfy all our desires. We may suffer loss of goods, loss of family, loss of the good functioning of heart and lungs, our legs and arms. But we know we will not want for anything we ought to want. For what we ought to want is to be one of your flocks, listening to your voice, obeying your prompting, glorifying you by showing your character in our lives. Lord, you are our shepherd! We shall not want!

[2]   He makes me lie down in green pastures;

Leader: Imagine the scene pictured in verses 2-4. Think of yourself as one of the shepherd's sheep. What do you want? What do you need? *(Pause; then pray:)* You, Lord Jesus, Word of God, feed us on your written Word—green pastures indeed, full of nourishment for body, mind and spirit.

he leads me beside still waters;

Leader: In this dry and decadent wasteland of popular culture, you slake our thirst for living water. Amidst the world of empty images, of ubiquitous TV and endless advertising of things for which there is no good use either practical or aesthetic, your presence satisfies our longing for genuine reality.

3   he restores my soul.

Leader: You restore our souls. You fill us with the delight of knowing you, of being puzzled by you and your ways, of seeing that we have yet to see so many things about you. We come to you as broken, distorted images of God, Lord, and you are repairing the damage and fitting us for life in your kingdom. Thank you, Lord! Thank you, Jesus! Oh that this restoration would proceed! There is so much more for you to do. Bring to mind some areas in your life that you know you need help in. *(Pause.)* May we be worthy sheep who bend to your leading!

He leads me in right paths
  for his name's sake.

Leader: You refocus our lives, you refine our goals, you head us in the right direction. And you do this not just for us but for the glory it brings to you, to the Father and to the Holy Spirit. Remind yourself, then tell the Lord, some of the specific ways he has directed you—in relationships, in job selection, in tough decisions. *(Pause.)*

4Even though I walk through the darkest valley,

> I fear no evil;
>   for you are with me;
>   your rod and your staff—
>   they comfort me.

Leader: Picture yourself as a sheep walking in a dark shadow, the shadow of the valley of death. See the dangers that lurk behind the rocks, the sheep stealers who want you for their flock and will kill to get you. *(Pause; then pray:)* We know that you do not take us out of the world. We are now and will be till the end immersed in the cares of the world. Money, sex and power continue to trouble us. Bring to mind some specific cares. *(Pause.)* But when we turn our attention to you, we realize that the evils of this world are nothing beside your power to save and comfort us. Like every one of your sheep, we have walked through some dark shadows. Name some of them and be specific. *(Pause.)* But you have been with us all along. Help us now to realize that at the most profound level of our soul.

> ⁵You prepare a table before me
>   in the presence of my enemies;
>   you anoint my head with oil;
>   my cup overflows.

Leader: Picture a rich feast, with the host having provided good things beyond your expectation. *(Pause; then pray:)* Lord, you give us such joy, even in the fallen world, even when forces we cannot control put pressure on us to disobey you and live by standards we know are wrong. You sustain us with your presence so that we can ignore those who would wish us ill. Think of some relevant examples from your life recently. *(Pause.)* Our cups overflow.

> ⁶Surely goodness and mercy shall follow me

all the days of my life,
and I shall dwell in the house of the LORD
my whole life long.

Leader: See your life spread out before you, now full of confidence and hope. *(Pause; then pray:)* Indeed, Lord, this is the substance of our hope. You are our shepherd. We hear your voice, and we know that you will be with us all of our days—and then throughout eternity. Amen.

8

RIDE ON, O KING ETERNAL

Psalm 45

As I read Psalm 45 recently, I was struck by the sudden appearance of the celebration of a royal wedding. For modern Americans such a poem is odd. The closest we have come to a regal wedding is having watched on TV the marriage of Prince Charles and Diana years ago. And that memory was eclipsed by their marital scandals, culminating in Diana's funeral service with pomp, circumstance, a full orchestra and Elton John singing "A Candle in the Wind."

Yet here in the Bible is a celebration of what seems a strictly human event. A handsome young king is marrying his beautiful bride in ancient Middle Eastern splendor. Both are charged with the task of ruling well and living rightly, but nothing is made of their connection to issues prominent either now or in New Testament times. Yet this wedding song has made it into the Hebrew Scriptures and then into the New Testament, with its ultimate fulfillment in Christ's marrying the church. How does this happen? And how can we pray such a psalm? We begin with the psalm itself.

Psalm 45

Ode for a Royal Wedding

To the leader: according to Lilies. Of the Korahites. A Maskil.
A love song.

   [1] My heart overflows with a goodly theme;
        I address my verses to the king;
        my tongue is like the pen of a ready scribe.

   [2] You are the most handsome of men;
        grace is poured upon your lips;
        therefore God has blessed you forever.
   [3] Gird your sword on your thigh, O mighty one,
        in your glory and majesty.

   [4] In your majesty ride on victoriously
        for the cause of truth and to defend the right;
        let your right hand teach you dread deeds.
   [5] Your arrows are sharp
        in the heart of the king's enemies;
        the peoples fall under you.

   [6] Your throne, O God, endures forever and ever.
        Your royal scepter is a scepter of equity;
   [7] you love righteousness and hate wickedness.
     Therefore God, your God, has anointed you
        with the oil of gladness beyond your companions;
   [8] your robes are all fragrant with myrrh and aloes and cassia.
     From ivory palaces stringed instruments make you glad;
   [9] daughters of kings are among your ladies of honor;
        at your right hand stands the queen in gold of Ophir.
   [10] Hear, O daughter, consider and incline your ear;

forget your people and your father's house,
[11]   and the king will desire your beauty.
   Since he is your lord, bow to him;
[12]   the people of Tyre will seek your favor with gifts,
      the richest of people [13]with all kinds of wealth.

   The princess is decked in her chamber with
         gold-woven robes;
[14]   in many-colored robes she is led to the king;
      behind her the virgins, her companions, follow.
[15]With joy and gladness they are led along
      as they enter the palace of the king.

[16]In the place of ancestors you, O king, shall have sons;
      you will make them princes in all the earth.
[17]I will cause your name to be celebrated in all generations;
      therefore the peoples will praise you forever and ever.

GETTING AT THE MEANING OF PSALM 45

What struck me first as I prepared to study and pray this psalm is how elegantly human it is. Psalm 45 is a love song, and it appears at first to be only that. God is, of course, mentioned, and the king is seen as his agent on earth, but the focus is on the king and his bride. Looked at in this way, the structure of the psalm is clear.

Rational Structure

The rational structure is straightforward and can be charted clearly without including the text itself.

   Invocation (eagerness to celebrate), verse 1

   Address 1 to the king (you are the greatest), verses 2-9

Address to the bride (you are the most beautiful), verses 10-13a

The procession (the bride comes to the king), verses 13b-15

Address 2 to the king (you will prosper), verses 16-17

The overall structure of the psalm is clear. First there is an introduction, then an address to the king, an address to the bride, a brief description of her procession to the king and finally a prophecy of an eternal future.

Read the psalm again with this structure clearly in mind, and visualize the scene, letting the imagery, pomp and ceremony sink in.

Start by noticing the exuberance of the bard. He is so full of his subject that it bursts forth. He can't just speak the lines, he must as a poet write them down. Then follow the moving picture he presents.

Observe the king. Not only is he handsome and arrayed in royal finery, but in character he is like God himself: he is the very picture of might, glory and majesty. He will be victorious in battle as he fights for truth and righteousness. With powerful weapons in hand he will fell all his enemies. Moreover, he will reign with equity and righteousness forever. God has so anointed him that his very bearing exudes the fragrance of glorious character. He is entertained by the Zion Philharmonic Orchestra and served in his court by the daughters of foreign kings. Before him stands his queen, bedecked in the finest gold. (Notice that in this paraphrase I have struggled for words. The psalm itself contains the best ones!)

Observe the bride now. She is beautiful—stunning—and dressed in a gold-woven dress, a wedding gown to end all wedding gowns. She comes to the king, like a modern bride to the church altar; trailing behind her are her bridesmaids, excited time out of mind by their role in this wedding to end all weddings. She is ready to leave her people and become the king's helpmate as she receives gifts of wealth from the surrounding nations.

The poet, his pen exhausted from its eloquence, then prophesies. O king, he says, forget your ancestors, look forward to your progeny. They will reign in splendor. They will not forget you, nor will all the future generations.

Some wedding song, this great paean of praise to the glorious king and queen of ancient Israel! And in our reflection on its deeper meaning, we should not think of it only as a garment for theological reflection but honor it, its poet, and the king and queen for whom it was composed, though we don't know who they were. Art is sometimes its own justification! Just being what it is—a royal wedding song—is enough. Without any transcendent signification, any deep meaning, any messianic implication, it stands as an emblem of finite aesthetic creativity and thus as a reflection of God's infinite creativity. In our attempt to internalize the psalm, let us not fail to internalize its blazing beauty. In our prayer we will try to give this its due.

Second Meanings

Nothing in the psalm itself points to any specific king's wedding that prompted the composition. This psalm could have applied to many royal weddings and probably was. Some scholars, such as John Calvin and Michael Wilcock, hold that the king is Solomon and the bride his first wife (1 Kings 3:1), but that move leads to some unhappy conundrums, not the least of which is that what is said of the king seems not to fit Solomon, a king who eventually had many wives and concubines. Rather than trying to untangle the problems associated with any guess about the identity of the king and his bride, we will treat the psalm as a generic royal wedding song.

We must not, however, neglect what C. S. Lewis called "second meanings." As Lewis pointed out, with a little imagination one can invent allegorical meanings from the most prosaic of texts. How much more so is this the case with poetry. But with Psalm 45 we have a precedent. As the writer of Hebrews cites several passages from the Old Testament to show that Jesus, the Son of God, is superior to the angels, he quotes Psalm 45:6-7.

> Of the angels [God] says,
>> "He makes his angels winds,
>>> and his servants flames of fire."
> But of the Son he says,
>> "Your throne, O God, is forever and ever,
>>> and the righteous scepter is the scepter of your kingdom.
>> You have loved righteousness and hated wickedness;
>> therefore God, your God, has anointed you
>>> with the oil of gladness beyond your companions."
> (Hebrews 1:7-9)

Where did the writer to the Hebrews get the idea that the king of Psalm 45 was and is in some sense Jesus Christ, the King of kings and Lord of lords? There was, of course, a long tradition in Jewish thought that the early kings, especially David, were a type of messiah. Psalm 110 shows that. And while "the direct meaning of those [royal] songs is concerned with the Israelite king as he reigned on earth," writes Pius Drijvers,

> the books of the New Testament are full of the interpretation [that Christ is found in the psalms], inspired by the love of Christ, of the old texts. No wonder that already the faithful in the early Church read into psalm 72 the description of the life of the Church, in psalm 21 they found the triumph of their king

described, and it psalm 45 they saw the glory of God's Son for whom the Church is as a bride (Eph 5:25-27), and in psalm 2 and 110 the might and victory of their Lord.

It is, however, in Psalm 45 itself that we find the root of the insight. The poet in verse 6 suddenly turns from addressing the king to addressing God (or to the king himself as God); then he immediately shifts back to the king, who has been anointed by "God, your God" (verse 7). Did the ancient poet nod off or speak amiss, or did he have insight beyond his normal senses? Or is the king as God no more divine than those angels and other mighty beings who are referred to as gods elsewhere in the Scriptures (Psalm 82:6; Isaiah 41:23; John 10:35)? Scholars disagree. But most of them see the propriety of a "second meaning," understanding Jesus Christ as fulfilling the role no human being could fulfill—the perfect King who in his righteousness wins all battles and embodies all the characteristics of God—and the church as reflected in the character of the new queen.

But once we see that a "second meaning" is to be found, just how should we develop our grasp of that meaning? One way taken by many preachers is to see Psalm 45 as line-by-line allegory, with many, if not every, detail in the picture of the king and queen finding its fulfillment in either Christ or the church. Examples of this can be cited almost without end. Here are a few:

- *You are the most handsome of men:* "In Jesus we behold every feature of a perfect character in harmonious proportion. He is lovely everywhere, and from every point of view, but never more so than when we view him in conjugal union with his church" (Spurgeon).

- *Your arrows are sharp:* "Nothing that Jesus does is ill done, he uses no blunted shafts, no pointless darts" (Spurgeon). And "the arrows which are discharged from the bow of Christ are the preachers of the gospel, especially the apologists and the evangelists" (Christopher Wordsworth).

- *Your robes are all fragrant with myrrh and aloes and cassia:* "The excellencies of Jesus are all most precious, comparable to the rarest spices; they are to be likened not to myrrh alone, but to all the perfumes blended in due proportion. . . . To attempt to spiritualise each spice here mentioned would be unprofitable, the evident sense is that all sweetnesses meet in Jesus, and are poured forth wherever he is present" (Spurgeon).

- *Forget your people and your father's house.* "By *her father's house* and *her people* is doubtless meant all the corruptions which we carry with us from our mother's womb, or derive from evil custom" (Calvin). Calvin, like Spurgeon, does, however, caution restraint in such allegorizing: "It is not necessary for us to examine every word minutely, in order to apply to the Church every thing here said concerning the wife of Solomon."

- *Behind her the virgins, her companions, follow:* "These are members of the church, but the figure of a bridal train is employed to sustain the allegory" (Duncan Macgregor).

We likewise could make our own list of allegorical correspondences. But that approach somehow seems hermeneutically wrongheaded. The psalm is not so much an allegory as an analogy. Details do not need to be spiritualized. Even Spurgeon and Calvin, who have contributed their share to this approach, admitted this, as we see above.

Still, we must not miss the fulfillment of this psalm in the character and mission of Jesus. So in our prayer we will try to combine the two levels. The king and the bride are both literal and analogical.

PSALM 45 IN THE LIFE OF CHRIST

What can we sense of the way Jesus read and experienced this psalm? Here we are on very thin ice. But we can think about it, if only to speculate. So long as we do not take ourselves too seriously, we may benefit from the exercise.

Jesus would have known this psalm simply by being in the community of faith. The curiosity he displayed at age twelve suggests that whatever he read in the Scriptures was probed and pondered. Imagine him reading this wedding song. Would he not see its hyperbole? No king had ever really been pictured as in Psalm 45. There were good ones and bad, corrupters of the faith and reformers, weak ones and strong. But there had never been a king who displayed the character of the king of this psalm.

Had Jesus had an ounce of the cynicism of a typical twenty-first-century English teacher, he would have deconstructed this psalm in a second. Who could be like this bride and groom? Come on, give me a break. The poet was just hoping to receive his commission! And what a picture of the relationship between commanding men and submissive women. Here is a poem affirming the decadent ideology of the ancients and moderns! We postmoderns know this is not the way anyone lived then or now or ever.

But while we know Jesus had no need to be taught about the weakness and evil of human nature, we also know he never treated anyone with contempt. He reserved his harshest judgment for those filled with obvious pretense. He made wine from water to help the host at a wedding, rather than point out the mismanagement that caused the problem in the first place.

So here he is facing this romantic psalm, a part of his religious heritage. Would he wonder, if there has been no one like this king and his bride, if there *could* be no one like this king and bride, why is this psalm in the Psalter? The monarchy is corrupt, a puppet of Rome. There is no reason for the psalm to have been preserved in the heart of the liturgy of faith. Did Jesus then remember that his people believed that Yahweh is the real king over Israel? The Israelites longed for an anointed one, a Messiah, a conqueror who would come to liberate Israel and set up the sort of kingly reign imagined and projected by this psalm. Was there not a positive way the psalm could be read? Who would be this genuine king? Did Jesus come to believe that Psalm 45 really depicted himself and the church? Did, perhaps, even the writer of the letter to the Hebrews get his own perception of the connection from something Jesus told the disciples in his postresurrection, preascension teaching?

One thing we can know. The early church soon came to see this. They found Jesus in Psalm 45.

PRAYING PSALM 45

Read through the psalm a couple of times to refresh your memory of the whole. Then pray:

Lord, help me as I try to put myself into the life of this psalm. I want to feel with the heart of the psalmist, see with the eyes of the ancient Israelites and perceive with the mind of your Son as he found himself in this psalm.

> [1]My heart overflows with a goodly theme;
>> I address my verses to the king;
>> my tongue is like the pen of a ready scribe.

Respond: My heart too overflows, for I know what the psalmist is going to say. I know how this prayer turns out. What I don't know is how well I will be able to pray it. Lord, help me feel what the psalmist felt and see what the early church saw in the king and queen.

²You are the most handsome of men;
    grace is poured upon your lips;
    therefore God has blessed you forever.
³Gird your sword on your thigh, O mighty one,
    in your glory and majesty.

*Respond: Picture in your own mind the image painted by the psalmist.
Pause.*

⁴In your majesty ride on victoriously
    for the cause of truth and to defend the right;
    let your right hand teach you dread deeds.

Respond: See the king astride a noble steed. Pause.

⁵Your arrows are sharp
    in the heart of the king's enemies;
    the peoples fall under you.

Respond: See him mighty in battle. Pause. Then pray: Lord, as I visualize
this scene and draw out its details in my imagination, let my mind
begin to contemplate the ways Jesus the Christ fulfills this vision. Let
me understand him triumphant over spiritual powers as he wrestles
not with flesh and blood but with the forces of evil and with those
who oppose his ways. *Pause.*

⁶Your throne, O God, endures forever and ever.
    Your royal scepter is a scepter of equity;
⁷   you love righteousness and hate wickedness.

Respond: Your throne, O God, is not the throne of an earthly king.
Your throne endures forever. You rule with equity; you love

righteousness and hate wickedness. And you desired this for earthly rulers as well! But these rulers failed Israel long ago, and our rulers fail us today. So like those in Jesus' day, we long for the peaceable kingdom of God. Praise to you, Lord, for we have hope that our longing will one day be satisfied and more.

> Therefore God, your God, has anointed you
>> with the oil of gladness beyond your companions;
> [8] your robes are all fragrant with myrrh and aloes and cassia.
> From ivory palaces stringed instruments make you glad;
> [9] daughters of kings are among your ladies of honor;
>> at your right hand stands the queen in gold of Ophir.

Respond: Picture this scene—the anointed king, the fragrance of spice, the orchestra, the daughters of foreign kings, the queen. Pause.

> [10]Hear, O daughter, consider and incline your ear;
>> forget your people and your father's house,
> [11] and the king will desire your beauty.
> Since he is your lord, bow to him;

Respond: Hear the psalmist address the bride; consider his advice to her. Pause. Lord, I hear the words spoken to the bride. I know that when Jesus is seen to be the king, the psalmist is addressing his bride, the church. And his advice is wise. May I forget my heritage in sin, my past deeds unworthy of you, my Lord. Lord, I bow before you. May I press on, looking forward to a life worthy of you.

> [12] the people of Tyre will seek your favor with gifts,
>> the richest of people [13]with all kinds of wealth.

Respond: The ancient queen may expect beautiful gifts from surrounding nations to flow to her. The church cannot expect this,

for we do not exhibit the ideal as she does. Grant us your favor, Lord.
That is enough.

> The princess is decked in her chamber with gold-woven
> > robes;
> 14   in many colored-robes she is led to the king;
> > behind her the virgins, her companions, follow.
> 15With joy and gladness they are led along
> > as they enter the palace of the king.

Respond: As I see the pageant unfold in the palace of the king, I also
see the church arrayed in robes of righteousness given by Christ. It is
being brought to Christ. Lord, we as the church, filled with joy, will
stand before you in glory as bride to groom. We anticipate that now
in this picture of a royal wedding. We are the bride of Christ.
Hallelujah!

> 16In the place of ancestors you, O king, shall have sons;
> > you will make them princes in all the earth.
> 17I will cause your name to be celebrated in all generations;
> > therefore the peoples will praise you forever and ever.

Respond: The reign of the Messiah-King is already present in this
world. There has never been a time when your praise was not offered
up by some—many—in the world. But we look forward to the
coming of your kingdom in its fullness, when every knee shall bow
and every tongue confess that Jesus Christ is Lord to the glory of the
Father. In the name of the Father and the Son and the Holy Spirit,
Amen.

SOME FURTHER REFLECTIONS

In addition to the royal psalms we have already studied and prayed

(2; 45; 110), there are several others: 20; 21; 72; 101 and 144. Each will add a dimension to our understanding of the faith of ancient Israel: "In the enthronement and royal psalms the psalmist sang of . . . future happiness, and looked forward to the reign of God, to the new king, to re-creation and salvation, to what Jeremiah calls 'the new and everlasting covenant,' the full communion with the Holy God." And if the early church has not misled us into a romantic allegorizing or analogizing of these ancient psalms, we get as well a glimpse of the inner life of Jesus.

Small Group Study of Psalm 45

The following comments are directed to the leader.

Group Questions

1. Have one person read Psalm 45 in its entirety at an ordinary pace.

2. Have another person read it very slowly, with a pause after each verse.

3. A third reading would be appropriate unless it looks as if people in the group are getting restless.

4. Note: Begin your study by focusing on the obvious literal meaning of the psalm. Turn to the New Testament only after this meaning is clear to participants. So ask: What is the main topic of this psalm? Does this seem like a psalm relevant to you and other Christians today? Why? (Participants may find this psalm odd in a book of "prayers" and think it irrelevant to them. Don't stifle such comments.)

5. Outline the flow of ideas. What are the major sections of the psalm? Who is being addressed in the various sections?

6. What are the characteristics of the king? What is praised about him? Are any faults mentioned?

7. Describe the bride. What is she advised to do? Why? How will she be treated by the king and the surrounding nations?

8. How is the wedding scene similar to and different from weddings today?

9. What does the future hold for the king?

10. Do you see any reason that this psalm should have been retained in the book of Psalms, especially after the exile in Babylon, when the reign of kings was either over or largely ineffective?

11. What hint do we have in the New Testament that Psalm 45 is relevant not only to ancient history but to Jesus' time and ours as well? Have someone read the entire first chapter of Hebrews. How does Hebrews 1:8-9 interpret the identity of the king?

12. What other "evidence" is there that Psalm 45 can be interpreted as applying to Jesus? Consider any negative evidence (if the literal meaning is the only meaning, no king of Israel ever did or ever could be the one who matched the description; also the prophecy of the final verses was never fulfilled).

13. How then does Jesus become the fulfillment of the psalm? How does the psalm fit him? Who is his bride?

14. Why then is this psalm relevant to the church today?

When you feel that the group is ready for corporate prayer, you may use the following liturgy.

Directed Prayer

Leader: Let us pray Psalm 45 together.

Lord, help us as we try to put ourselves into the life of this psalm. We want to feel with the heart of the psalmist, see with the eyes of the ancient Israelites and perceive with the mind of your Son as he found himself in this psalm.

> [1]My heart overflows with a goodly theme;
>> I address my verses to the king;
>> my tongue is like the pen of a ready scribe.

Leader: Our hearts too overflow, for we know what the psalmist is going to say. We know how this prayer turns out. What we don't know is how well we will be able to pray it. Lord, help each of us feel what the psalmist felt and see what the early church saw in the king and queen.

> [2]You are the most handsome of men;
>   grace is poured upon your lips;
>   therefore God has blessed you forever.
> [3]Gird your sword on your thigh, O mighty one,
>   in your glory and majesty.

Leader: Picture in your own mind the image painted by the psalmist. *(Pause.)*

> [4]In your majesty ride on victoriously
>   for the cause of truth and to defend the right;
>   let your right hand teach you dread deeds.

Leader: See the king astride a noble steed. *(Pause.)*

> [5]Your arrows are sharp
>   in the heart of the king's enemies;
>   the peoples fall under you.

Leader: See the king mighty in battle. *(Pause.)* Lord, as we visualize this scene and draw out its details in our imagination, let us begin to contemplate the ways Jesus the Christ fulfills this vision of the Israelite king. Let us understand him triumphant over spiritual powers as he wrestles not with flesh and blood but with the forces of evil and with those who oppose his ways. *(Pause.)*

> [6]Your throne, O God, endures forever and ever.
>   Your royal scepter is a scepter of equity;
> [7]   you love righteousness and hate wickedness.

Leader: Your throne, O God, is not the throne of an earthly king. Your throne endures forever. You rule with equity; you love righteousness and hate wickedness. And you desired this for earthly rulers as well! But Israel's rulers failed that nation long ago, and our rulers fail us today. So like those in Jesus' day, we long for the peaceable kingdom of God. Praise You, Lord, we have hope that our longing will one day be satisfied and more. *(Pause.)* Now we turn back to the psalmist and his words about the ancient king.

> Therefore God, your God, has anointed you
> > with the oil of gladness beyond your companions;
> 8   your robes are all fragrant with myrrh and aloes and cassia.
> From ivory palaces stringed instruments make you glad;
> 9   daughters of kings are among your ladies of honor;
> > at your right hand stands the queen in gold of Ophir.

Leader: Picture this scene—the anointed king, the fragrance of spices, the orchestra, the daughters of foreign kings, the queen. *(Pause.)*

> 10Hear, O daughter, consider and incline your ear;
> > forget your people and your father's house,
> 11   and the king will desire your beauty.
> Since he is your lord, bow to him;

Leader: Hear the psalmist address the bride; consider his advice to her. *(Pause.)* Lord, we hear the words spoken to the bride. We know that when Jesus is seen to be the king, the psalmist is addressing his bride, the church. And his advice is wise. May we forget our heritage in sin, our past deeds unworthy of your bride. O Lord, our Lord, we bow before you. May we press on, looking forward to a life worthy of you.

> 12   the people of Tyre will seek your favor with gifts,
> > the richest of people 13with all kinds of wealth.

Leader: The ancient queen may expect beautiful gifts from surrounding nations to flow to her. The church cannot expect this, for we do not exhibit the ideal as she does. Grant us your favor, Lord. That is enough.

> The princess is decked in her chamber with gold-woven
> robes;
> ^{14} in many-colored robes she is led to the king;
> behind her the virgins, her companions, follow.
> ^{15}With joy and gladness they are led along
> as they enter the palace of the king.

Leader: Watch the pageant unfold in the palace of the king. *(Pause.)* Now see the church, arrayed in robes of righteousness given by Christ, processing to a great heavenly wedding feast. Lord, may we see ourselves in this pageant! Lord, we as the church, filled with joy, will stand before you in glory as bride to groom. We anticipate that now in this picture of a royal wedding. We are the bride of Christ. Hallelujah!

> ^{16}In the place of ancestors you, O king, shall have sons;
> you will make them princes in all the earth.
> ^{17}I will cause your name to be celebrated in all generations;
> therefore the peoples will praise you forever and ever.

Leader: The reign of the Messiah-King is already present in this world. There has never been a time when your praise was not offered up by some—many—in the world. But we look forward to the coming of your kingdom in its fullness, when every knee shall bow and every tongue confess that Jesus Christ is Lord, to the glory of the Father. In the name of the Father and the Son and the Holy Spirit, Amen.

How Long, O Lord, Will You Be Angry?

Psalm 80

Longing is a universal emotion. We long for all sorts of things—better health, a new car, better relationships with our spouse, our children, our friends, our fellow workers, a more peaceable world, a bigger apartment, cooler clothes. But Jesus laid aside all concern for these human but often trivial desires and concentrated on matters of central importance—the plight of his people, who had deliberately turned away from the answer to their deepest need.

After teaching and healing, Jesus entered Jerusalem. When he was told that Herod wanted to kill him, he said with great but frustrated compassion, "Jerusalem, Jerusalem, the city that kills the prophets and stones those who are sent to it! How often have I desired to gather your children together as a hen gathers her brood under her wings, and you were not willing!" (Luke 13:34).

Would Jerusalem ever repent and turn again to the God whom he revealed by being the very Son of God incarnate? We know that Jesus' desire has yet to be satisfied.

The ancient Hebrews, too, longed for the salvation of Israel. "How

long, O Lord?" is a phrase that appears over and over in the psalms.
Sometimes it is linked with personal anguish: "How long, O LORD?
Will you forget me forever?" (Psalm 13:1). Sometimes it is even more
plaintive because the lament is broken off from completion:

> My soul also is struck with terror,
>> while you, O LORD—how long? (Psalm 6:3)

At other times the cry rises concerning the fate of the Hebrew people as a nation. That is the case in Psalm 80. The corporate nature of
this lament prompts interesting reflections on how Jesus would have
responded. We have already seen how he adopted the personal lament of Psalm 22 for his own. How would he relate to the corporate
lament of Psalm 80? How can we do the same? The answers will
make a fitting close to the present collection of psalms.

PSALM 80

Prayer for Israel's Restoration

To the leader: on Lilies, a Covenant. Of Asaph. A Psalm.

> ¹Give ear, O Shepherd of Israel,
>> you who lead Joseph like a flock!
> You who are enthroned upon the cherubim, shine forth
> ² before Ephraim and Benjamin and Manasseh.
> Stir up your might,
>> and come to save us!

> ³Restore us, O God;
>> let your face shine, that we may be saved.

> ⁴O LORD God of hosts,
>> how long will you be angry with your people's prayers?

⁵You have fed them with the bread of tears,
  and given them tears to drink in full measure.
⁶You make us the scorn of our neighbors;
  our enemies laugh among themselves.

⁷Restore us, O God of hosts;
  let your face shine, that we may be saved.

⁸You brought a vine out of Egypt;
  you drove out the nations and planted it.
⁹You cleared the ground for it;
  it took deep root and filled the land.
¹⁰The mountains were covered with its shade,
  the mighty cedars with its branches;
¹¹it sent out its branches to the sea,
  and its shoots to the River.
¹²Why then have you broken down its walls,
  so that all who pass along the way pluck its fruit?
¹³The boar from the forest ravages it,
  and all that move in the field feed on it.

¹⁴Turn again, O God of hosts;
  look down from heaven, and see;
  have regard for this vine,
¹⁵ the stock that your right hand planted.
¹⁶They have burned it with fire, they have cut it down;
  may they perish at the rebuke of your countenance.
¹⁷But let your hand be upon the one at your right hand,
  the one whom you made strong for yourself.
¹⁸Then we will never turn back from you;
  give us life, and we will call on your name.

¹⁹Restore us, O LORD God of hosts;

    let your face shine, that we may be saved.

GETTING AT THE MEANING OF PSALM 80

Author

Most of the psalms attributed to Asaph (50 and 73—83) involve the people of Israel as a nation. We know a little about Asaph: he was "a descendant of Gershom, son of Levi (1 Ch. 6:39); nominated by the chief Levites as a leading singer, using cymbals, when the Ark was brought to Jerusalem (1 Ch. 15:17, 19). David made him leader of the choral worship (16:4-5)."

His descendants remained involved in the music services until the Israelites returned from exile in Babylon. From the psalms attributed to him (or his descendants) it is clear that he was interested in the status of Israel in relation to God and the surrounding nations. All of his psalms wrestle with why the Israelites have strayed and, worse, why God is taking so long to restore them to his favor.

I have found it difficult to pick only one of Asaph's psalms to study and pray. To catch something of the total effect of the Asaph insights and puzzlements, I suggest that you read all of his psalms before you attempt to pray Psalm 80. It is a task worth both the effort and the time.

Historical Setting

It is especially helpful to see Psalm 80 in its historical context. The great unified kingdom of Israel, which seemed to fulfill the promises God made to his people, stretched from Sinai ("the mountains") in the south to Lebanon ("the mighty cedars") in the north and the Mediterranean ("the sea") in the west to the Euphrates ("the River") in the east. This vast empire had been ruled by David (1011-971 B.C.) and reached its peak under Solomon (1070-945 B.C.). Soon after Solomon's reign it split into two. Then in 722 B.C. Assyria captured the northern kingdom (Israel), represented in Psalm 80 by three of the ten tribes (Ephraim, Benjamin and Manasseh) that constituted the northern nation. After 722 B.C. these tribes dispersed into the surrounding area and ceased to have an independent existence. With the fall of Jerusalem in 587 B.C., the southern kingdom (Judah) was also obliterated, and most of the inhabitants were taken into exile in Babylon.

Psalm 80, then, is a lament for what was left of national identity after the first or perhaps the second of these two catastrophes. It assumes both a great loss and a betrayal of the true goal for the reign of David and his descendants.

This psalm has complex intertwining layers of structure, each of which contributes to the overall effect of the psalm: There are rational, rhetorical, emotional and image structures. We will take them up in turn.

Rational Structure

The flow of ideas is not difficult to determine.

Invocation (to God as shepherd), verses 1-2

Prayer/refrain 1 (restore us, O God), verse 3

Lament 1 (how long will you be angry with us?), verses 4-6

Prayer/refrain 2 (restore us, O God), verse 7

Lament 2 (to God as viticulturist), verses 8-13

Prayer/refrain 3 (have regard for us, O God), verses 14-15

Lament 3 (continued), verse 16

Longing (for a Messiah-King), verses 17-18

Prayer/refrain 4 (restore us, O God), verse 19

Rhetorical Structure

The psalm develops in a nice literary rhythm:

invocation
   prayer
lament
   prayer
lament
   prayer
lament
   prayer
lament
   solution to the lament
   prayer

Emotional Structure

Its emotional structure is also interesting:

Positive but plaintive plea from the heart, verses 1-3

Negative complaint, sadness, discouragement, verses 4-6

Positive, plaintive plea/refrain, verse 7

Negative complaint, memory of a time of prosperity, verses 8-13

Positive plea/variation on the refrain, verses 14-15

Angry, desperate call for stern judgment on the nation's enemies, verse 16

Positive vision for a solution and hope for the future, verses 17-18

Positive plea/refrain, subdued, chastened hope, verse 19

Image Structure

In this psalm Yahweh is seen first as *shepherd,* then as *light* in the sense that he is "enthroned [as *king*] upon the cherubim," and finally as *viticulturalist.*

We have seen the *shepherd* image before, of course, in Psalm 23. It is a common image of God as guide and protector of the flock, the Hebrew people. As Christians we have little difficulty understanding this image, especially as it triggers thoughts of Jesus as the Good Shepherd.

The image of God as *light* enthroned on "the cherubim" (the ark of the covenant) needs some explanation. "The ark was a rectangular box . . . made of acacia wood, and measured . . . 4½ x 2½ x 2½ feet. . . . The whole was covered with gold and was carried on poles inserted in rings at the four lower corners. The lid, or 'mercy seat,' was a gold plate surrounded by two antithetically-placed cherubs with outspread wings." The ark contained the two tables of the Ten Commandments, a pot of manna and Aaron's rod. It symbolized the providential history of the Hebrew people and the power and presence of God as lawgiver and guide. In Psalm 30, the psalmist calls on God first to shine forth from the mercy seat and shed light on the northern kingdom, then to come in all his power to save "us" (presumably the southern kingdom and perhaps what remains of the people of the northern kingdom after its demise). The image of God as light is then extended into the refrain (verses 3, 7, 19): God is to shine on all his people.

With the image of God as *viticulturalist* the psalmist pictures God uprooting the vine of the Hebrew people. The vine had been firmly planted (enslaved) in Egypt, but God had reset it in the Promised Land, where it grew so tall and abundant that it shaded the whole unified kingdom of David and Solomon—south to the mountains of Sinai, north to Lebanon, west to the Mediterranean and east to the Euphrates. Then the image darkens, and the psalmist accuses God of breaking down the boundaries to this gigantic vineyard and letting the surrounding nations ravage the vineyards and forests.

These three images of God express the frustration of the psalmist. The great kingdom is split and then mostly destroyed. What has happened? What else will happen? Will God be the shepherd who leads his flock? Will he again shine his face on his people? Will he restore his vineyard? Or will the seemingly endless destruction continue? The psalmist's plea is desperate and relentless.

> Restore us, O God;
>> let your face shine, that we may be saved. (verses 3, 7, 19)

And

> Turn again, O God of hosts;
>> look down from heaven, and see;
>> have regard for this vine,
>> the stock that your right hand planted. (verses 14-15)

Psalm 80 is truly an anguished national lament. But it is a lament that is intended to inspire hope. The psalmist has a solution in mind. He dreams—no, envisions—a Messiah, one who because of his closeness to God can deliver the people.

> But let your hand be upon the one at your right hand,
>> the one whom you made strong for yourself.

Then we will never turn back from you;
  give us life, and we will call on your name. (vv. 17-18)

Did the Asaph psalmist know how God would finally answer this plea? Did he hope for a king soon to come who would reclaim the area lost to the Assyrians, reunite it with Judah and reestablish the Davidic empire? Or did he somehow get a tiny glimpse of the way God would redeem and restore his people through Jesus? Was he like Abraham, who, Jesus said, "rejoiced that he would see my day; he saw it and was glad" (John 8:56)?

PSALM 80 IN JESUS

Think about the psalm from Jesus' standpoint. Here was an ancient lament, a psalm that focused attention on the nation in crisis. The promises of God seemed not to be fulfilled. The Jews were no longer under the reign of a king from the line of David. They had been under the thumb of surrounding nations for hundreds of years. Now they were under the heel of Rome. First-century Israel again desperately needed God's help if it was to realize the promises.

So when Jesus read the psalm—when he absorbed its words and participated in its grief—did he find himself there? Did he see himself as the one seated at the right hand of God? That seems likely, for by the time he left the wilderness and began his ministry, he saw his mission as realizing the hope of ancient Israel. In one of his early commentaries on Isaiah, for example, he claimed that he himself was the one Isaiah had in mind (Luke 4:16-21).

We know that the psalm itself was in Jesus, for he knew the Scripture better than anyone before him. We also believe, along with the church down through the ages, that Jesus himself is, by the fulfillment of its vision, very much in this psalm.

PRAYING PSALM 80

Read through the psalm a couple of times to refresh your memory of the whole.

Then pray: I know that this psalm displays the agony of Asaph or his descendant as he saw the destruction of his nation. And I know that Jesus could well have seen himself as the solution to the longing heart of the psalmist and his nation. Lord, lead me as I pray.

> [1]Give ear, O Shepherd of Israel,
>> you who lead Joseph like a flock!

Respond: I pause here to make these words of the psalmist my own. Give ear, O Good Shepherd of ancient Israel. Give ear to the present sheep of your pasture. Give ear to the church, give ear to me, a single sheep in your flock. Lead me in your way as I pray.

> You who are enthroned upon the cherubim, shine forth
> [2] before Ephraim and Benjamin and Manasseh.

Respond: You who shine on your people in Israel and around the world, shine on me and my nation.

> Stir up your might,
>> and come to save us!

> [3]Restore us, O God;
>> let your face shine, that we may be saved.

Respond: I plead for your presence as Shepherd, Lord and Savior. *Pause.*

> [4]O LORD God of hosts,
>> how long will you be angry with your people's prayers?

⁵You have fed them with the bread of tears,
    and given them tears to drink in full measure.
⁶You make us the scorn of our neighbors;
    our enemies laugh among themselves.

Respond: I hear the psalmist as he laments the fall of the northern kingdom. I sympathize with him and the people he represented so many years ago. But I too have been fed with the bread of tears, and I too sometimes feel that you are angry with my prayers and the prayers of my friends. At times I feel the scorn of those who think we Christians are stupid or even malicious as we place our faith in you and support the causes they despise. *Pause; bring to mind current illustrations of this in your own life, and lay them before God.*

I long for your acceptance of my prayers. I long to feel reconciled to you. You seem so far away.

⁷Restore us, O God of hosts;
    let your face shine, that we may be saved.

Respond: O Lord, bring us, bring me, relief. Lift me up. Shine, Jesus, shine. Shine on me. *Pause.*

⁸You brought a vine out of Egypt;
    you drove out the nations and planted it.
⁹You cleared the ground for it;
    it took deep root and filled the land.
¹⁰The mountains were covered with its shade,
    the mighty cedars with its branches;
¹¹it sent out its branches to the sea,
    and its shoots to the River.
¹²Why then have you broken down its walls,
    so that all who pass along the way pluck its fruit?

¹³The boar from the forest ravages it,
>   and all that move in the field feed on it.

Respond: Lord, you raised up David and Solomon; you fulfilled your promises to your people. Then the nation split. Then the northern kingdom fell, and the psalmist laments it. The southern kingdom fell too, and hope for the political independence of your people was all but dashed. *Pause to let this sink into your consciousness.*

¹⁴Turn again, O God of hosts;
>   look down from heaven, and see;
>   have regard for this vine,
> ¹⁵   the stock that your right hand planted.
> ¹⁶They have burned it with fire, they have cut it down;
>   may they perish at the rebuke of your countenance.

Respond: I hear the psalmist plead again for salvation for the nation. May you, Lord, answer my plea for restoration. *Bring and lay before God personal and communal petitions for God's good care.*

I hear, too, the psalmist's call for vengeance. I understand why he made this plea. Surely there should be judgment on those who destroy your people and degrade the dignity of your human creation. But I plead for them to recognize their sins. May they truly repent and receive your grace.

¹⁷But let your hand be upon the one at your right hand,
>   the one whom you made strong for yourself.
> ¹⁸Then we will never turn back from you;
>   give us life, and we will call on your name.

Respond: What a change in tone here! The psalmist has a solution! Hallelujah! There was one at his right hand who could solve the situation. Hope filled the psalmist's breast. He knew that the deliverer would come from God himself. Jesus too knew that as he came to see himself as the Messiah, the one to deliver not only the Hebrew people but the whole world. You give us life! We call on your name! Oh, Lord, save us from our own foolish generation! As you save us from our sinful selves, our longing is changed to rejoicing. Our "how long, O Lord," is changed to "How great you are!"

> [19]Restore us, O LORD God of hosts;
>> let your face shine, that we may be saved.

Respond: Thank you, Lord! Your salvation from the power of evil has already come in Jesus. Your salvation from the presence of evil will come. For that we have hope, even more than hope. We have assurance in your word and in our hearts. Even so, come, Lord Jesus!

SOME FURTHER REFLECTIONS

The psalms of Asaph (50 and 73—83) provide a fascinating insight into how the ancient Israelites dealt with national glory and devastation. Why not reread these psalms and pray them in the light of Psalm 80? It will deepen your appreciation both of the psalms and of the Lord who stands ready to save but whose salvation, mostly because of our sins, sometimes seems a long time coming.

Small Group Study of Psalm 80

The following comments are directed to the leader.

Group Questions

1. Have one person read Psalm 80 in its entirety at an ordinary pace.

2. Have another person read it very slowly, with a pause after each verse.

3. A third reading would be appropriate unless it looks as if people in the group are getting restless.

4. Did any of you find the psalm difficult to understand? What don't you understand? (Let the conversation reveal what needs clarifying. Then explain the historical context and the nature of the problem the psalmist was facing. See pp. 190-91 for details. If you wish to take a lot more time than usual for these prayer sessions, you could have several participants privately read other psalms of Asaph, then report to the group on what they see as similarities and differences with Psalm 80.)

5. How is God pictured in the psalm? (Be sure that the three images used of God—shepherd, light from the ark and viticulturalist—are understood.)

6. Have someone outline the flow of ideas of the psalm?

   What is the main problem the psalmist addresses? Where, if at all, does he find a possible solution?

7. How do you think Jesus might have understood the psalm.

   Why do you think he would have seen himself in verses 17-18?

8. Though firmly set in the history of Israel and in the life and mission of Jesus, in what ways does it speak to our nation?

When you feel that the group is ready for corporate prayer, you may use the following liturgy.

Directed Prayer

Leader: This psalm displays the agony of Asaph or his descendant as he saw the destruction of his nation. We believe that Jesus saw himself as the solution to the longing heart of the psalmist and his nation. Lord, guide us as we pray.

> [1]Give ear, O Shepherd of Israel,
>> you who lead Joseph like a flock!

Leader: We pause here to make these words of the psalmist our own. Give ear, O Good Shepherd of ancient Israel. Give ear to the present sheep of your pasture. Give ear to the church, give ear to us, this small herd of sheep in your flock. Lead us in your way as we pray.

> You who are enthroned upon the cherubim, shine forth
> 2   before Ephraim and Benjamin and Manasseh.

Leader: You who shone on your people in Israel and around the world, shine on us.

> Stir up your might,
>> and come to save us!

> [3]Restore us, O God;
>> let your face shine, that we may be saved.

Leader: We plead for your presence as Shepherd, Lord and Savior. (*Pause.*)

> [4]O LORD God of hosts,
>> how long will you be angry with your people's prayers?
> [5]You have fed them with the bread of tears,
>> and given them tears to drink in full measure.

⁶You make us the scorn of our neighbors;
       our enemies laugh among themselves.

Leader: We hear the psalmist as he laments the fall of the northern kingdom. We sympathize with him and the people he represented so many years ago. But we too have been fed with the bread of tears, and we too sometimes feel that you are angry with our prayers and the prayers of our friends. At times we feel the scorn of those who think we Christians are stupid or even malicious as we place our faith in you and support the causes they despise. Now, as individuals, bring to mind current illustrations of this in your own life and lay them before God. *(Pause.)*

We long for your acceptance of our prayers. We long to feel reconciled to you. You seem so far away.

⁷Restore us, O God of hosts;
       let your face shine, that we may be saved.

Leader: O Lord, bring each of us relief. Lift us up. Shine, Jesus, shine. Shine on us. *(Pause.)*

⁸You brought a vine out of Egypt;
       you drove out the nations and planted it.
⁹You cleared the ground for it;
       it took deep root and filled the land.
¹⁰The mountains were covered with its shade,
       the mighty cedars with its branches;
¹¹it sent out its branches to the sea,
       and its shoots to the River.
¹²Why then have you broken down its walls,
       so that all who pass along the way pluck its fruit?
¹³The boar from the forest ravages it,

and all that move in the field feed on it.

Leader: Lord, you raised up David and Solomon; you fulfilled your promises to your people. Then the nation split. Then the northern kingdom fell, and the psalmist laments it. The southern kingdom fell too, and hope for the political independence of your people was all but dashed. (*Pause to let this sink into each person's consciousness.*)

¹⁴Turn again, O God of hosts;
    look down from heaven, and see;
  have regard for this vine,
¹⁵ the stock that your right hand planted.
¹⁶They have burned it with fire, they have cut it down;
    may they perish at the rebuke of your countenance.

Leader: We hear the psalmist plead again for salvation for the nation. May you, Lord, answer our plea for restoration. Bring and lay before God personal and communal petitions for God's good care. (*Pause.*)

We hear, too, the psalmist's call for vengeance. We understand why he made this plea. Surely there should be judgment on those who destroy your people and degrade the dignity of your human creation. Recall who some of these are today. (*Pause.*) But we plead that they would recognize their sins. May they truly repent and receive your grace.

¹⁷But let your hand be upon the one at your right hand,
    the one whom you made strong for yourself.
¹⁸Then we will never turn back from you;
    give us life, and we will call on your name.

Leader: What a change in tone here! The psalmist has a solution!

Hallelujah! There was one at God's right hand who could solve the situation. Hope filled the psalmist's breast. He knew that the deliverer would come from God himself. Jesus also knew that as he came to see himself as the Messiah, the one to deliver not only the Hebrew people but the whole world.

Lord, you give us life! We call on your name! Oh, Lord, save us from our own foolish generation! As you save us from our sinful selves, our longing is changed to rejoicing. Our "how long, O Lord," is changed to "How great you are!"

[19]Restore us, O LORD God of hosts;

let your face shine, that we may be saved.

Leader: Thank you, Lord! Your salvation from the power of evil has already come in Jesus. Your salvation from the presence of evil will come. For that we have hope, even more than hope. We have assurance in your Word and in our hearts. Even so, come, Lord Jesus!

A FINAL WORD

I suggest that you encourage participants to read the Asaph psalms (50 and 73—83) and pray them on their own.

EPILOGUE

Apologetics and the Psalms of Jesus

My study of the psalms of Jesus has had an unexpected benefit for me. I had no idea that I would find that even the psalms can contribute to Christian apologetics.

Many apologists have tried to justify Christian faith by the ways that Jesus and the events of history have fulfilled Old Testament prophecy. I have never tried to do this. The gaps between the so-called predictive messianic prophecies and their supposed fulfillment in Jesus has always seemed too large for me. A skeptic could find it easy to attribute the seeming fulfillment to clever manipulation of Old Testament texts by the writers of the New Testament. The Gospel writers had already decided that Jesus had fulfilled the prophecies, so they inserted Old Testament allusions into the Gospels. Clever Christians, especially apologists, have found more of these allusions in the Gospels than even the writers themselves put there. They have simply built into their interpretation all that is needed to draw the conclusions they want. Or so I have thought. But when I looked at the psalms from the standpoint of how Jesus himself understood them, I discovered profound connections I had not seen before.

Take Psalm 22, for instance. When Jesus from the cross quoted not only the first verse ("My God, my God, why have you forsaken me?") but probably also alluded to the last one ("It is finished"), it was obvious that he was deliberately linking himself not only to the agony of the psalmist but to the psalmist's ecstasy in the final verses. Only if Jesus is the Messiah, the one sent by God to complete the salvation of the world by his death on the cross, do these final verses make sense. Only because Jesus triumphed over death should everyone in the whole world—the living and the dead, the rich and poor, then and now and for all time—experience the rejoicing that ends the psalm. The psalm's allusions to mocking, bones out of joint, casting lots for his clothes, heart melting like wax, dry mouth—all these suggest that this psalm depicts more than its composer or even Israel itself ever knew.

Then, too, take Psalm 110. Jesus says that he is the one who sits at the right hand of God (verse 1), implying as well that he is also "a priest forever according to the order of Melchizedek" (verse 4). Surely if this is not true, then Jesus is more than mildly deluded. He is a blasphemer worthy of condemnation, not a Savior worthy of the greatest honor and praise. So his reading of Psalm 110 gives fuel to the trilemma argument.

This argument rests on the premise that anyone who claims to be God (or, as I would reframe the argument, anyone who claims, as Jesus did, to "sit at the right hand of God" or "be a priest according to the order of Melchizedek") is a liar, a lunatic or the Lord himself. He was not a liar; that belies the testimony of the whole of every Gospel. He was not a lunatic; that too does not fit with Jesus' preeminent ability to function fully and sanely in society. Therefore, he was and is the Lord.

Add to this Psalm 118, which Jesus used to respond to the Pharisees' challenge to his authority. He claimed that he was the "stone that the builders rejected," the one who would form the foundation of a new temple. Jesus was replacing the sacrificial system of the old covenant. Anyone who is wrong about that is not making just a little mistake. He is undermining not only his authority as a religious teacher but his sanity as a human being. Again, he would be making a case for his own damnation and for that of all who believed him.

Other of the psalms help us see into the mind of Jesus, making us aware of the fullness of his humanity. He was not a divine ethereal being who existed on earth as a mere shadow of a man. With flesh and blood he tasted all the wine of humanity—the dry and the sweet, the sour and the spoiled. He understood the deepest level of human sin and degradation, the highest heights of human goodness and glory. He absorbed the reality the psalmists displayed in their agony and ecstasy. Jesus' four last words from the cross clinch the argument: He was and is the man for all ages and eternity, the risen Lord, to whom we say, "Even so, come, Lord Jesus!"

APPENDIX

Guide for Small Group Leaders

Small groups can learn to pray through the psalms. The procedure is similar to that of private prayer but takes place in community. Solitude is gone, but silence is still possible. Moreover, there is the added factor that when two or three are gathered together, Christ is there with you.

Learning to pray through the psalms does, of course, make demands on the group leader. The following suggestions should smooth the way to successful group experiences and spiritual growth for those who participate.

1. Come to the group prepared. Make this psalm your own answering speech. That is, work through the material in each chapter a few days before the group meets. This will give your experience with the psalm time to confirm itself in your own life.

2. Just before the group meets, review the relevant chapter and then answer the study questions preceding the group prayer liturgy. As you do so, imagine the sorts of answers and comments group

members are likely to give. This anticipation will help you to handle any tough issues that may arise.

3. Be willing to participate in the discussion. You will not be lecturing; instead you will be encouraging the members of the group to discuss what they have seen in the psalm.

4. Be sensitive to the other members of the group. Listen attentively when they describe what they are seeing. You may be surprised by their insights. Most questions do not have a single "right" answer. This is especially true of those relating to application or to personal experiences.

When possible, link what you say to the comments of others. Also, be affirming whenever you can. This will encourage some of the more hesitant members of the group to participate.

5. Be careful not to dominate the discussion. We are sometimes so eager to express our thoughts that we leave too little opportunity for others. By all means participate, but encourage all others to do so as well.

6. When you lead the prayer, speak slowly and pause when a pause is called for. The silence that follows may be more important to the spiritual experience of the members than the time you are speaking. At first this silence may feel awkward to the members. Let them know that silence is important. With repeated experiences as you proceed through the psalms, the silence will feel less and less awkward. Participants may eventually tell you that the silences following the words of the psalm are the richest moments of the prayer.

7. Expect God to teach you through the psalm and through the preceding conversation among group members.

8. Comments made during the study will often reveal personal matters that are confidential and should not be discussed outside the group unless specific permission is given to do so. This should be made clear to the group at the beginning of each study.

9. At the end of the group prayer liturgy, some may want to say something about their personal experience. Give them freedom and time to do so. These comments may reveal personal problems. Let these comments spark practical responses that can be made in the next few days and weeks.

I have led many groups and been a participant in many more. I can say with confidence that if you as a leader give heart and mind to personal study and prayer, you will be greatly rewarded by what you see happening in the lives of those who participate. May God give you great joy in serving him by helping others!

NOTES

INTRODUCTION

page 12   Their answering speech becomes: Eugene Peterson, *Answering God* (San Francisco: HarperSanFrancisco, 1991), p. 54.

page 12   "for there is not an emotion": John Calvin, "The Author's Preface," in *The Psalms of David and Others*, trans. Henry Beveridge, Calvin's Commentaries 4 (Grand Rapids: Baker, 2003), p. xxxvii. Tremper Longman III's "The Psalms: Mirror of the Soul," in *How to Read the Psalms* (Downers Grove, Ill: InterVarsity Press, 1988), pp. 76-85, fleshes out this notion.

page 13   Likewise during the Last Supper: For scholarly justification for this reading of these psalms, see R. T. France, *Jesus and the Old Testament* (Downers Grove, Ill.: InterVarsity Press, 1971), pp. 55-60. See also Longman, *How to Read the Psalms,* pp. 63-68.

page 13   They became his answering speech: Peterson, *Answering God,* p. 54.

page 15   "In some of the Psalms": C. S. Lewis, *Reflections on the Psalms* (London: Collins, 1961), p. 23.

page 15   "He was willing to undergo": Thomas C. Oden, *The Word of Life,* vol. 2 of *Systematic Theology* (San Francisco: Harper & Row, 1989), p. 224.

page 15   "the Psalter took its final form": Graeme Goldsworthy, *Preaching the Whole Bible as Scripture: The Application of Biblical Theology to Expository Preaching* (Grand Rapids: Eerdmans, 2000), p. 199.

page 16   "he is recorded": Goldsworthy adds: "As well as indicating that Jesus himself constantly used the Psalms, the Gospel writers use and apply the Psalms in their account of Jesus and his ministry. A number of times events are seen as the fulfillment of prophecy in the Psalms: for example Matthew 13:35 quotes Psalm 78:2 as fulfilled; John 19:24 fulfills Psalm 22:18; and John 19:36 fulfills Psalm 34:20" (ibid.).

page 16   "It is hard to say": Ben Witherington III, *The Christology of Jesus* (Minneapolis: Fortress, 1990), pp. 185-86.

page 16   "All Old Testament texts": Goldsworthy, *Preaching the Whole Bible,* p. 198.

page 17   "It is the incarnate Son of God": Dietrich Bonhoeffer, *Psalms: The Prayer Book of the Bible* (Minneapolis: Augsburg, 1970), pp. 20-21.

page 18   In part one: Strictly speaking, Jesus did not directly refer to Psalm 2, but the early church did so with gusto.

CHAPTER 1: JESUS, ABANDONED AND EXALTED

page 23   "There is an infinite abyss": Slightly paraphrased from Blaise Pascal, *Penseés,* trans. A. J. Krailsheimer (Harmondsworth, U.K.: Penguin, 1966), no. 148, p. 75.

page 23   "Our heart is restless": Saint Augustine, *Confessions,* trans. Henry Chadwick (Oxford: Oxford University Press, 1991), p. 3.

page 28   Scholars generally believe: Michael Wilcock, *The Message of Psalms 1–72,* The Bible Speaks Today (Downers Grove, Ill.: InterVarsity Press, 2001), pp. 24-26, 81-82.

page 29   In fact, the whole psalm: I owe the notion that "he has done it" (v. 31) prefigures "It is finished" (John 19:3) to Charles C. H. Spurgeon, *The Treasury of David* (Peabody, Mass.: Hendrickson, n.d.), 1:334; few other scholars seem to have noticed this. But Wilcock does say, "From start to finish 22 could have been uttered by him, with truth and passion, at Calvary" (Wilcock, *Message of Psalms 1–72,* p. 241).

page 34   "It is absolutely safe": Richard Dawkins made this frequently quoted (and criticized) statement in a book review in the *New York Times,* April 9, 1989. His rejoinder criticism can be found in "Ignorance Is No Crime" in *Free Inquiry Magazine* 21, no. 3, or at <www.secular humanism.org/library/fi/dawkins_21_3.html>. He comments, "Of course it *sounds* arrogant, but undisguised clarity is easily mistaken for arrogance. Examine the statement carefully and it turns out to be moderate, almost self-evidently true." Dawkins then explains why, adding "tormented, bullied and brainwashed" into the mix of causes that some do not believe the evolutionary story. The notion, however, that his outrageous statement is "almost self-evidently true" illustrates the power of Dawkins's own commitment to the evolutionary theory; it does not show the statement to be "almost self-evidently true," nor does the remainder of his essay "Ignorance Is No Crime."

CHAPTER 2: A KING AND PRIEST FOREVER

page 49   "was destined to form": Derek Kidner, *Psalms 73–150: A Commentary on Books III-V of the Psalms,* Tyndale Old Testament Commentary (Downers Grove, Ill.: InterVarsity Press, 1975), p. 393.

page 49   "pray this psalm we must": Stanley Jaki, *Praying the Psalms: A Commentary* (Grand Rapids: Eerdmans, 2001), p. 195.

page 50   If Jesus himself: One view, taken by Leslie C. Allen, is that the psalm is primarily a royal psalm (or "enthronement psalm"). The speaker of the opening lines is a "court poet" who is celebrating the exaltation of David to be king of Israel centered in Jerusalem by declaring that God himself has appointed David (v. 1) and will give him a strong reign (vv. 2-3). The court poet then declares that God has also made David a priest after the mysterious order of Melchizedek (v. 4) and adds that, at God's right hand, he will triumph over his enemies (vv. 5-7). The problem with this view is that it conflicts with Jesus' declaration that the speaker of the opening line is David himself. It also raises the question whether Psalm 110 is messianic, a view that was not only that of Jesus but of the rabbis of his time and the church down through the ages. To solve these problems and dissolve the seeming contradiction between Jesus' interpretation (accepted by the apostles and early church) and that of modern scholars like Allen, one can understand Jesus as seeing himself as a fuller embodiment of King David, a "fulfillment," if you will, of the *full* implications of this enthronement. That is, Jesus is both the eternal King and the eternal Priest. In slightly more technical terms. David is the *type* and Jesus is the *antitype*, the one toward whom the psalm is intended by the Holy Spirit, if not the original court poet, to point. (See Leslie C. Allen, *Psalms 101–150*, Word Biblical Commentary 22 [Waco, Tex.: Word, 1983], pp. 78-87.)

page 51   "Our Lord gave full weight": Kidner, *Psalms 73–150*, p. 392.

page 51   I will take my cue: In doing this, I will in general be following the lead of Kidner, *Psalms 73–150*; Jaki, *Praying the Psalms*; and R. T. France, *Jesus and the Old Testament* (Downers Grove, Ill.: InterVarsity Press, 1971), pp. 100-102, 163-69; rather than that of Allen, *Psalms 101–150*, 78-87.

page 52   the first-century rabbis: Jaki, *Praying the Psalms*, pp. 195-96; see also France, *Jesus and the Old Testament,* pp. 164-67.

page 55   "The Messianic dominion": France, *Jesus and the Old Testament*, p. 103.

page 55   Rather, he is the Messiah: Ibid., p. 101.

page 56   But if the premise of this book: Christopher J. H. Wright says about Jesus
               and the Old Testament, "For these are the words he read. These were the
               stories he knew. These were the songs he sang. These were the depth of
               wisdom and revelation and prophecy that shaped his whole view of 'life,
               the universe and everything.' This is where he found his insights into the
               mind of his Father God. Above all, this is where he found the shape of
               his own identity and the goal of his own mission. In short, the deeper
               you go into understanding the *Old Testament*, the closer you come to the
               heart of Jesus" (*Knowing Jesus Through the Old Testament* [Downers
               Grove, Ill.: InterVarsity Press, 2001], p. ix). Wright provides an excellent
               detailed summary and analysis of the Old Testament passages that af-
               fected Jesus' self-understanding most (pp. 55-180).

pages 56-57 Then comes his time: See Wright, *Knowing Jesus*, pp. 183-87, for a
               clear exposition of Jesus' temptation by Satan.

page 57   "Jesus never mentioned": As France says, "We have no case in the Syn-
               optic Gospels of his accepting either [title, *Son of Man* or *Messiah*] with-
               out such reinterpretation, in terms of either Daniel 7:13, Isaiah 53,
               Zechariah 9:9 or Psalm 110:1" (France, *Jesus and the Old Testament*, p.
               103).

CHAPTER 3: THE STONE THE BUILDERS REJECTED

page 73   without digging in: Michael Wilcock, *The Message of Psalms 73–150*,
               The Bible Speaks Today (Downers Grove, Ill.: InterVarsity Press,
               2001), p. 189.

page 73   One way to open the entire psalm: There are a variety of ways to iden-
               tify the speakers of the various lines. A priest may open the psalm with
               invitations to praise (vv. 1-4), and he or another could be the speaker
               of verse 26, for example. Though I have made some additions and
               changes, in general I am following Wilcock's sense of the structure of
               the ritual/liturgy (ibid., pp. 189-90). See as well Leslie C. Allen, *Psalms
               101–150*, Word Biblical Commentary 21 (Waco, Tex.: Word, 1983),
               pp. 124-25.

page 75   The lector pauses: Wilcock says, "We can only guess to whom it would
               fall to say the momentous words of verse 22" (Wilcock, *Message of*

Psalms 73–150, p. 190). I have guessed that it is the lector, who represents the king.

page 76   "Bind the festal procession": The action directed by this verse is obscure. Suffice it to say that NRSV translation indicates that those in the procession are to perform a ritual action involving the "horns of the altar," that is, "the projections at each of the four corners of the altar" (*Harper's Bible Dictionary,* ed. Paul J. Achtemeier [San Francisco: Harper & Row, 1985], p. 405).

page 78   Jesus saw himself: "The cornerstone is the principal stone around which construction in antiquity was achieved. In the lexicon of biblical images of architecture, no image is more evocative than the cornerstone, the focal point of a building, the thing on which it most depends for its structural integrity" (Leland Ryken, James C. Wilhoit and Tremper Longman III, *Dictionary of Biblical Imagery* [Downers Grove, Ill.: InterVarsity Press, 1998], p. 166).

CHAPTER 4: YOU ARE MY SON

page 97   The kings of the surrounding nations: The translation of the phrase "kiss his feet" or "kiss the son" is contested by scholars. If the NRSV is correct, the idea is for the kings of the nation to submit to Yahweh. If the NIV translation "kiss the Son" is correct, then the foreign kings are to acknowledge the primary kingship of David and his line. I have followed the NRSV in my comments. But see, for example, Peter C. Craigie, *Psalms 1–50,* Word Biblical Commentary 19 (Waco, Tex.: Word, 1983), p. 64; Derek Kidner, *Psalms 1–73,* Tyndale Old Testament Commentary (Downers Grove, Ill.: InterVarsity Press, 1972), pp. 52-53.

page 98   The text is generic: Craigie, *Psalms 1–51,* pp. 65-66.

pages 98-99 neither Psalm 2: As Pius Drijvers says, none of these psalms points to a future figure who "is concerned with the final redemption of man, and also with the king of those last days who will bring about the redemption. . . . An accurate analysis of the royal psalms has proved for certain that nowhere can we find in them any trace of the last king of all who will reign at the end of time. They are concerned with the earthly kings of David's line and not with the person of the Messiah" (*The Psalms: Their Structure and Meaning* [New York: Herder and Herder, 1964], pp. 198-99).

page 99   Primarily the royal psalms: The term *son of God* in the Old Testament
                 is not used to signify divinity or transcendence. When that notion is
                 expressed, the term *son of man* carries this weight. See Daniel 7.

page 99   "Everything foretold": Drijvers, *Psalms,* p. 181.

page 102   "Given this family of citations": It will not matter to our reading of
                 Psalm 2 whether the apostle is envisioning the events of the end time
                 yet to come or to the way God was judging Rome. Either way, Psalm 2
                 is absorbed into his conception of the great acts of God's judgment of
                 the nations.

CHAPTER 5: ZEAL FOR YOUR HOUSE

page 119   "From start to finish": Michael Wilcock, *The Message of Psalms 1–72,*
                 The Bible Speaks Today (Downers Grove, Ill.: InterVarsity Press,
                 2001), p. 241.

page 121   so unsavory are these metaphors: Marvin E. Tate writes, "The language
                 of these verses is harsh and need not be repeated here" (*Psalms 51–100,*
                 Word Biblical Commentary 20 [Waco, Tex.: Word, 1990], p. 199).

page 121   "In some of the Psalms": C. S. Lewis, *Reflections on the Psalms* (London:
                 Collins/Fontana, 1958), p. 23.

page 122   "The enemies referred to": Dietrich Bonhoeffer, *Psalms: The Prayer
                 Book of the Bible* (Minneapolis: Augsburg, 1970), p. 57.

page 123   "Jesus Christ himself requests": Ibid., p. 59.

page 126   "I love you more than": Eugene H. Peterson, *The Message: Psalms* (Col-
                 orado Springs: NavPress, 1994), p. 97.

CHAPTER 6: HE RIDES UPON THE STORM

page 143   Second, notice how: Scholars disagree on just how to read and trans-
                 late the phrase "sons of gods" in the Hebrew text. Along with Derek
                 Kidner, Michael Wilcock and Peter Craigie, the NRSV takes it to mean
                 "heavenly beings," that is, "angels" or "the divine counsel" or "heavenly
                 court." John Calvin holds that the phrase is ironic: they think they are
                 big stuff, but they are only the arrogant princes of the earth who need
                 to be put in their place. Charles Spurgeon, seeing less irony, calls them
                 the "great ones of the earth and of heaven, kings and angels," and Sir
                 Philip Sidney calls them "men of power (even by birth-right)." See Pe-
                 ter C. Craigie, *Psalms 1–50,* Word Biblical Commentary 19 (Waco,

Tex.: Word, 1983), p. 246; Derek Kidner, *Psalms 1–72,* Tyndale Old Testament Commentary (Downers Grove, Ill.: InterVarsity Press, 1972), p. 125; Michael Wilcock, *The Message of Psalms 1–72,* The Bible Speaks Today (Downers Grove, Ill.: InterVarsity Press, 2001), p. 101; John Calvin, *The Psalms of David and Others: Commentary on the Book of Psalms,* trans. James Anderson (Grand Rapids: Baker, n.d.), 1:475-76; Charles Spurgeon, *The Treasury of David* (Peabody, Mass.: Hendrickson, n.d.), 1:29; and *The Psalms of Sir Philip Sidney and the Countess of Pembroke,* ed. J. C. A. Rathmell (Garden City, N.Y.: Anchor, 1963), p. 62.

page 144   This psalm has also prompted: See the comments collected by Charles C. H. Spurgeon in *The Treasury of David,* 1:29-42.

page 144   "He is portrayed": Craigie, *Psalms 1–50,* p. 247.

page 145   "the deified *flood*": Ibid., p. 249.

page 145   Philosophers have so separated God: "Philosophers think not that they have reasoned skilfully enough about inferior causes, unless they separate God very far from his works. It is a diabolical science, however, which fixes our contemplations on the works of nature, and turns them away from God. If any one who wished to know a man should take no notice of his face, but should fix his eyes only on the points of his nails, his folly might justly be derided. But far greater is the folly of those philosophers, who, out of mediate and proximate causes, weave themselves veils, lest they should be compelled to acknowledge his works" (Calvin, *Psalms,* p. 479). See also Spurgeon, *Treasury,* p. 30.

page 147   "God does not need": Karl Barth, *The Faith of the Church: A Commentary on the Apostle's Creed According to Calvin's Catechism,* trans. Gabriel Vahanian (New York: Living Age, 1958), p. 27.

page 147   To glorify God: Barth says, "Created to glorify God, we must know God so that we may and can glorify Him. . . . To glorify God, to live according to God, is hence a conscious act, an act of the will; in a word, a human act" (ibid., p. 28).

CHAPTER 7: THE LORD IS MY SHEPHERD

page 157   Some have wondered if the host: See Phillip Keller, *A Shepherd Looks at Psalm 23* (Grand Rapids: Zondervan, 1970). Keller overemphasizes the details of sheepherders and their sheep and draws spiritual lessons that derive more from his overelaboration than from solid literary anal-

page 158

ysis. Still, he grounds his understanding of the psalm in the nitty-gritty life of real sheep ranching.

The psalm works magic: There is one issue, however, which I don't think would arise were it not for the comments of C. S. Lewis. He sees this change of image as a radical shift from the pleasant to the grotesque, from praise of God to imprecation of the psalmist's enemies. "In some of the psalms the spirit of hatred which strikes us in the face is like the heat from a furnace mouth. [Lewis cites several apt illustrations.] Worst of all in 'The Lord is my shepherd' (23), after the green pastures, the waters of comfort, the sure confidence in the valley of the shadow, we suddenly run across (5) 'Thou shalt prepare a table for me *against them that trouble me*'—or, as Dr. Moffat translates it, 'Thou art my host, spreading a feast for me *while my enemies have to look on.*' The poet's enjoyment of his present prosperity would not be complete unless those horrid enemies (who used to look down their noses at him) were watching it all and hating it. . . . The pettiness and vulgarity of it, especially in such surroundings, are hard to endure."

The best excuse we can offer for Lewis's lapse here is to notice that he has relied not on the standard translations of Psalm 23, attested to by a host of scholars, but on one by Moffat, an individual scholar who has probably misread the psalm. Was Lewis so bent on showing the ghastliness of the imprecatory sections of the psalms that he needed his pièce de résistance to be the most loved of all psalms? Would not that show the pervasiveness of cursing throughout the Psalter? Or shall we rather say of Lewis what one wag said of occasional ineptitude in the *Iliad* and the *Odyssey*, "Even Homer nods"?

But let us not nod. The psalmist is not cursing his enemies. Rather he is blessing God for taking full care of him even when he is beset by nearby enemies who want to kill him. The Lord as shepherd and the Lord as host work together to bring comfort.

CHAPTER 8: RIDE ON, O KING ETERNAL

page 174

They will not forget you: There is a distinct possibility that verses 16-17 are meant to be in the voice of the Lord himself. Frequently in royal psalms an oracle, a transcendent voice, prophesies or reveals a deep truth. We have already seen that in Psalms 2 and 110. If this is so, then the last section of the psalm should be labeled "The Lord addresses the king: (you will prosper)."

page 175   "second meanings": C. S. Lewis, *Reflections on the Psalms* (London: Fontana, 1961), pp. 84-91.

page 175   "the direct meaning of those [royal] songs": Pius Drijvers, *The Psalms: Their Structure and Meaning* (New York: Herder and Herder, 1964), p. 197.

page 176   "In Jesus we behold": Charles C. H. Spurgeon, *The Treasury of David* (Peabody, Mass.: Hendrickson, n.d.), 1:316.

page 176   "Nothing that Jesus does": Ibid., 1:317.

pages 176-77 "the arrows which are discharged": Christopher Wordsworth, quoted in ibid., 1:328.

page 177   "The excellencies of Jesus": Ibid., 1:318-19.

page 177   "It is not necessary": John Calvin, *The Psalms of David and Others: Commentary on the Book of Psalms,* trans. James Anderson (Grand Rapids: Baker, n.d.), 1:189-90.

page 177   "These are members of the church": Duncan Macgregor, quoted in Spurgeon, *Treasury,* 1:335.

page 183   "In the enthronement": Drijvers, *Psalms,* p. 208.

CHAPTER 9: HOW LONG, O LORD, WILL YOU BE ANGRY?

page 189   The ancient Hebrews: In eight different psalms the psalmist directs his complaint to God; in two psalms God directs his complaint to his people.

page 192   Most of the psalms attributed to Asaph: Michael Wilcock says, "The compilers [of the Psalter] have gathered Asaph psalms, all with a recognizable family likeness, from widely spaced points in history. From perhaps 1000 BC comes 78; from 701 BC, 75 and 76; from 587 BC, 74 and 77 and 79. Now with 80 the destruction of Ephraim, Benjamin, and Manasseh in 722 BC seems in view" (*The Message of Psalms 73–150,* The Bible Speaks Today [Downers Grove, Ill.: InterVarsity Press, 2001], p. 35).

page 192   "a descendant of Gershom": J. P. U. Leiley, "Asaph," in *New Bible Dictionary,* ed. D. R. W. Wood et al., 3rd ed. (Downers Grove, Ill.: InterVarsity Press, 1966), p. 91.

page 192   It is especially helpful to see Psalm 80: Scholars differ in their estimates of the specific time this psalm was composed, but it is clear that it reflects on the situation of the nation after the fall of the northern kingdom, some say even a time after the Babylonian exile. See Marvin E. Tate, *Psalms 51–100,* Word Biblical Commentary 20 (Dallas: Word, 1990), pp. 309-13.

page 193   Then in 722 B.C.: Scholars have expressed a variety of explanations of the three tribes that are listed in verse 2. Only two (Ephraim and Manasseh) of the ten tribes of the northern kingdom (Israel) are mentioned. Benjamin was a "buffer state," usually considered as part of the southern kingdom (Judah). After puzzling over this issue, Wilcock concludes, "It is natural to suppose that Benjamin was one of the ten, and belonged in principle if not always in fact to the north (1 Kgs. 15:22)" (*Message of Psalms 73–150,* p. 33n).

page 195   "The ark was a rectangular box": K. A. Kitchen, "The Ark of the Covenant," in *New Bible Dictionary,* ed. D. R. W. Wood et al., 3rd ed. (Downers Grove, Ill.: InterVarsity Press, 1966), p. 80.

BIBLIOGRAPHY

COMMENTARIES
The following commentaries are listed in the order I found most helpful in preparing this book.

Wilcock, Michael. *The Message of Psalms 1–72* and *The Message of Psalms 73–150*. The Bible Speaks Today. Downers Grove, Ill.: InterVarsity Press, 2001.

Kidner, Derek. *Psalms 1–72* and *Psalms 73–150*. Tyndale Old Testament Commentaries. Downers Grove, Ill.: InterVarsity Press, 1973 and 1975.

Allen, Leslie C. *Psalms 101–150*. Word Biblical Commentary 22. Waco, Tex.: Word Books, 1983.

Craigie, Peter C. *Psalms 1–50*. Word Biblical Commentary 19. Waco, Tex.: Word Books, 1983.

Tate, Marvin E. *Psalms 51–100*. Word Biblical Commentary 20. Waco, Tex.: Word Books, 1990.

BOOKS ON THE PSALMS
Drijvers, Pius. *The Psalms: Their Structure and Meaning*. New York: Herder and Herder, 1964.

France, R. T. *Jesus and the Old Testament*. Downers Grove, Ill.: InterVarsity Press, 1971.

Lewis, C. S. *Reflections on the Psalms*. London: Collins, 1961.

Longman, Tremper, III. *How to Read the Psalms*. Downers Grove, Ill: InterVarsity Press, 1988.

Peterson, Eugene. *Answering God*. San Francisco: HarperSanFrancisco, 1991.

Spurgeon, Charles C. H. *The Treasury of David*. 3 vols. Peabody, Mass.: Hendrickson, n.d.

Peterson, Eugene. *The Message: Psalms*. Colorado Springs: NavPress, 1994.

JESUS AND THE PSALMS

Brueggemann, Dale A. "The Evangelists and the Psalms." In *Interpreting the Psalms: Issues and Approaches,* edited by David Firth and Philip S. Johnston. Downers Grove, Ill.: InterVarsity Press, 2005.

Goldsworthy, Graeme. *Preaching the Whole Bible as Scripture: The Application of Biblical Theology to Expository Preaching.* Grand Rapids: Eerdmans, 2000.

Witherington, Ben, III. *The Christology of Jesus.* Minneapolis: Fortress, 1990.

PRAYER AND THE PSALMS

Bonhoeffer, Dietrich. *Psalms: The Prayer Book of the Bible.* Minneapolis: Augsburg, 1970.

Merton, Thomas. *Praying the Psalms.* Collegeville, Minn.: Liturgical Press, 1956.

Moore, T. M. *God's Prayer Program: Passionately Using the Psalms in Prayer.* Ross-shire, Scotland: Christian Focus Publications, 2005.

———. *The Psalms for Prayer.* Grand Rapids: Baker Books, 2002.

Sire, James. *Learning to Pray Through the Psalms.* Downers Grove, Ill.: InterVarsity Press, 2005.

formatio
TRADITION. EXPERIENCE.
TRANSFORMATION.

Formatio books from InterVarsity Press follow the rich tradition of the church in the journey of spiritual formation. These books are not merely about being informed, but about being transformed by Christ and conformed to his image. Formatio stands in InterVarsity Press's evangelical publishing tradition by integrating God's Word with spiritual practice and by prompting readers to move from inward change to outward witness. InterVarsity Press uses the chambered nautilus for Formatio, a symbol of spiritual formation because of its continual spiral journey outward as it moves from its center. We believe that each of us is made with a deep desire to be in God's presence. Formatio books help us to fulfill our deepest desires and to become our true selves in light of God's grace.